NEIL YOUNG

STORIES BEHIND THE SONGS 1966–1992

Nigel Williamson

CARLTON
BOOKS

THIS IS A CARLTON BOOK

This edition published by Carlton Books Limited
20 Mortimer Street
London W1T 3JW

ISBN 978-1-84732-694-2

Printed in China

CONTENTS

FOREWORD

I first encountered Neil Young in the Bromley High Street branch of W.H. Smith's, one rainy Saturday in early 1969. In those days, record stores had proper, sound-proofed listening booths with padded seats and it was here as young teenagers, with only the paper-round money to spend on records, that we sampled the cream of late 1960s rock'n'roll.

That afternoon – on the recommendation of Pete Badham, who always seemed to know what was hip long before the rest of us – we asked to hear *Everybody Knows This Is Nowhere*. The shop would only play one side before they threw you out. But it didn't matter. By then "Cinnamon Girl" and "Down By The River" had convinced me to buy the album on the spot.

I stayed faithful to Neil throughout the 1970s, eagerly buying every record on the day of its release, avidly following the reviews of his albums and concerts in *Melody Maker*, *Sounds* and *NME* and learning all the songs on the guitar rather badly. Then during the 1980s, Young's work disappeared off at a tangent and my life settled into a different pattern of domesticity, career and parenthood. I lost interest for a while, before we were reunited in 1988 and all was forgiven with the release of the excellent *This Note's For You*.

Throughout this period, I had to buy my own records, like most normal people. I didn't start writing about music for a living until 1995. Not long after, I got to meet Neil Young for the first time. It was a deflating experience. I had flown from London to San Francisco to see him and was given the last slot at the end of a long, exhausting day of interviews. We exchanged a few words before he announced, "I can't do this now, man. I'm really tired. Can you come to New York next week and we can talk then?" I couldn't, of course. But he flew in to London a few weeks later and we reconvened in a suite at his Park Lane hotel. He was full of apologies for the aborted interview and was friendly and charming. Yet he was mostly vague and uninformative about his songs.

CRAZY HORSE – NEIL YOUNG'S ALLIES FOR MORE THAN THREE DECADES.

In a way, I was rather glad. You don't really want Neil Young to blurt out his entire life story and to explain every intimacy of his songs line by line. He writes to express a feeling or an emotion or an experience – and if the meaning is ambiguous or unclear, then that's all part of the song's essential mystery. Yet there's endless fun in trying to unravel the mystery for ourselves, or at least place it in context. Hence this book.

J.D Salinger once said that to take from one source is plagiarism, but to borrow from many sources is research. In which case, this book can at least claim to be well-researched, if nothing else. The work of Young's several biographers all provided invaluable source material, although I must single out one in particular. Johnny Rogan's magisterial, 700-page *Neil Young – Zero To Sixty* is a work of both immense scholarship and passionate opinions which will uplift, inform and intimidate anyone who dares to write about Neil Young for years to come. Respect, Johnny.

Special thanks are also due to Allan Jones and all at *Uncut*; Peter Hall, not only a diligent head of press but a good friend; Ginny Luckhurst; my splendid editors Lorna Russell and Sarah Larter; Steve Cross for tracking down rare and otherwise unavailable recordings and to Pete Badham. Where are you now? My youngest son Piers Williamson contributed valuable computer assistance. But above all, thanks for everything go out to Magali Williamson. At the risk of sounding like a character from *High Fidelity* who measures out his life in album schedules, *On The Beach* had just been released when we met 28 years ago and she's been my "Cowgirl In The Sand" ever since.

Nigel Williamson

THE BUFFALO SPRINGFIELD YEARS

BUFFALO SPRINGFIELD (1966)

Musicians Buffalo Springfield: Richie Furay (guitar, vocals), Dewey Martin (drums, vocals), Bruce Palmer (bass), Stephen Stills (guitar, keyboards, vocals), Neil Young (guitar, harmonica, piano, vocals).

NOWADAYS CLANCY CAN'T EVEN SING
FLYING ON THE GROUND IS WRONG
BURNED
DO I HAVE TO COME RIGHT OUT AND SAY IT?
OUT OF MY MIND

BUFFALO SPRINGFIELD AGAIN (1967)

Musicians Buffalo Springfield *(as above)*.

MR SOUL
EXPECTING TO FLY
BROKEN ARROW

LAST TIME AROUND (1968)

Musicians Buffalo Springfield *(as above)* plus Jim Messina (bass, vocals).

ON THE WAY HOME
IT'S SO HARD TO WAIT (co-written with Richie Furay)
I AM A CHILD

BUFFALO SPRINGFIELD TAKE FIVE DURING A 1968 RECORDING SESSION.

When the Buffalo Springfield were inducted into the Rock and Roll Hall of Fame in 1997 almost 30 years after the group had broken up, Neil Young looked back with enormous affection.

"The music Buffalo Springfield made, the times we had, will always be an important part of my life," he noted. "I will always be grateful for coming of age during the mid-sixties and it still means as much to me, now and forever. I close my eyes, breathe deeply, open my soul and dream of the Buffalo Springfield."

He declined to attend in person, making his comments in a fax to his former colleagues and perhaps time had caused him to don a pair of rose-tinted spectacles. Buffalo Springfield was, in many ways, a deeply troubled group. During its brief two-year existence, the band was riven by personality clashes and repeated crises as Young and Stephen Stills jockeyed for supremacy within the group. The volatile Young walked out on at least two occasions before the Springfield finally broke up for good – he subsequently branded all of the group's three officially released albums as "failures". During his time with the Springfield, Young was also troubled by epileptic seizures, which often occurred on stage. Years after the group had broken up, he told his father, "I know I should have been happy, but in some ways it was the worst time of my life."

Yet over the years the Springfield's reputation and influence has grown dramatically. Whenever the group's name is mentioned today, it invariably comes accompanied by words such as "pioneering" and "seminal". Despite the tantrums and the egos and the bust-ups for which the band became notorious, Young's affection for the Springfield era and its music is clearly both profound and genuine.

Formed in early 1966 after the 18-year-old, Toronto-born Young and his friend and bassist Bruce Palmer had famously driven in a 1953 black Pontiac hearse from Canada to find Stills in Los Angeles, Buffalo Springfield was named after a steamroller they had spotted on the road. "Wouldn't it be really groovy if we ever got as big as that steamroller?" somebody allegedly joked.

The name stuck and the group played its first major gig supporting the Byrds in April 1966. They went on to become the house-band at the legendary Hollywood club, the Whisky A Go-Go, and with a line-up that in addition to Stills, Young and Palmer, boasted drummer Dewey Martin and Richie Furay, a fine singer and songwriter in his own right, they had an American top ten hit in early 1967 with Stills' memorable "For What It's Worth".

However, although they were hailed in many quarters as America's answer to the Beatles, they were never able to repeat that record's commercial success. None of the group's LPs even dented the top 40 and by the time the third and final album – appropriately titled *Last Time Around* – was released in October 1968, Buffalo Springfield had already ceased to exist.

BUFFALO SPRINGFIELD (FROM LEFT TO RIGHT): RICHIE FURAY, DEWEY MARTIN, BRUCE PALMER, STEPHEN STILLS AND NEIL YOUNG.

Nevertheless, they left behind a legacy of memorable songs, including a dozen top-drawer Young compositions. The group's importance was eventually commemorated in 2001 with the release of a lavish, four-CD box set, which included demos of a number of previously unreleased Young songs.

NOWADAYS CLANCY CAN'T EVEN SING

Released in January 1967, the first Springfield album included seven Stills compositions and five by Young. "Nowadays Clancy Can't Even Sing" was one of the album's most striking songs. One of Young's earliest efforts, he had first recorded it solo in November 1965, as an audition demo for Elektra Records on a trip to New York.

Elektra, which already had on its books such folk troubadours as Tom Paxton, Phil Ochs and Tom Rush, was underwhelmed and failed to sign him. But the trip was to have important repercussions. Young had met Stills earlier in the year when the latter had visited Ontario. The two had hit it off and Stills had invited Young to stay at his Greenwich Village apartment if he was ever in New York. When Young took him up on his offer six months later, Stills had already relocated to Los Angeles with the idea of putting together a rock'n'roll band. But his friend Richie Furay was in residence and made Young feel welcome during his three-day stay. Young played him "Clancy" and Furay was soon performing the song at auditions at Greenwich Village clubs such as The Bitter End.

Some months later, Young, Stills and Furay came together in LA with bass player Bruce Palmer and drummer Dewey Martin to form Buffalo Springfield. When it came to record the first album, Young's hesitancy as a singer meant that Furay took the lead vocal on "Clancy" with Stills singing harmony. "They had already learned it and they could sing it great. They were really good singers," Young later said.

Released as the band's first single in July 1966, the song was originally planned as the B-side to Stills' "Go and Say Goodbye", but the two tracks were flipped at the last minute, apparently at the insistence of Atlantic/Atco boss Ahmet Ertegun, who heard something different and appealing in Young's complex, introspective lyric and the track's attractive folk-rock arrangement.

It was a misjudgement. "Clancy" was an ambitious song to aim at the top ten and it reached only a disappointing No. 110 in the *Billboard* chart.

There was also some minor controversy over its use of the word "damn" but this was not the reason for its commercial failure – Young can only recall one radio station that objected, and even they merely bleeped out the offending word rather than refusing to play the record.

There has been much speculation over the identity of "Clancy" but the literal answer is simple enough. Ross "Clancy" Smith was an old Winnipeg school-mate who Young has described as "a kind of persecuted member of the community". Expanding on Clancy's character, he added, "He was a strange cat. Beautiful. Kids in school called him a weirdo... after a while he got so self-conscious he couldn't do his thing anymore."

But the song is also clearly autobiographical with Young strongly identifying with the notion of a free spirit whose non-conformist creativity is misunderstood by those around him. "The song's about me. And you," he added enigmatically to the magazine *Teen Set*. He also admitted that part of the song was "about my hang-ups with an old girlfriend back in Winnipeg." The song's theme of alienation became a familiar staple of some of his best early work.

FLYING ON THE GROUND IS WRONG

With three songwriters in the group, there was always going to be competition over whose songs the Springfield recorded. Richie Furay's "My Kind Of Love" had originally been intended for inclusion on the group's first album and even appeared on an early record company copy. Then, on September 10, 1966, late in the album sessions, Young came up with a new song. Furay's composition was unceremoniously dumped in its favour, with the result that he failed to get a single writing credit on *Buffalo Springfield*.

The song was "Flying On The Ground Is Wrong" and although Young had recorded a demo featuring just his own guitar, there was some consolation for Furay in that he was asked to take the lead vocal, one of three Young songs he sings on the album. The composer's original demo eventually surfaced many years later on the Buffalo Springfield box Set.

A beautiful, evocative song, it's easy to see the lyrics as typical of the drug-influenced imagery popular at the time. But the song is also notable as the first of Young's many meditations on the nature of fame and its effect on his fragile psyche.

BURNED

"Burned" was a turning point in Young's career, a fact that he recognized when it was one of the few Springfield tracks he chose to include ten years later on the career retrospective, *Decade*. "My first vocal ever done in a studio, late 1966," he remarked in the hand-written liner notes to the 1977 compilation. "The boys gave me some uppers to get my nerve up. Maybe you can hear that. I was living in a $12.50 per week apartment at the time and everybody on the floor liked it, too. We stayed up all night listening to it."

"NEIL'S LYRICS WERE FAR SUPERIOR TO MINE. HIS SONGS WERE LIKE POEMS IN A WAY, WHILE I USUALLY GOT STRAIGHT TO THE POINT."
STEPHEN STILLS

Richie Furay was bitterly disappointed not to sing the lead vocal, as he did on many of Young's early songs. But although by his own admission Young was "paranoid" about his voice, Dickie Davis, the group's road manager, recalls that he fought hard to sing "Burned". "Neil wasn't singing anything but background harmonies at the time," he says. "But he started pushing more and more for lead positions in vocals, justifying it by saying, 'I wrote the song and nobody else can sing it.'" The song was released as a single and when it failed to chart, some blamed Young's insistence on taking the vocal.

The song itself has a Byrds-type feel, with Young on piano as well as guitar and a typically ambiguous lyric full of references to coming down, confusion, flashing and crashing, which could be about drugs, fame or his epileptic seizures – or all three at once.

DO I HAVE TO COME RIGHT OUT AND SAY IT

"Back in the Springfield days, Neil's lyrics were far superior to mine. His songs were like poems in a way, while I usually got straight to the point," Stills later conceded. "Do I Have To Come Right Out And Say It", from the debut Springfield album, was perhaps the exception, a straightforward song about the uncertainty of starting a new love affair. Again, Furay took the lead vocal in a style that today sounds slightly mannered, while Young and Stills contribute some beautiful, almost baroque-sounding harmonies. Young soon came to disregard the song and has never seen fit to revive it during his solo years.

OUT OF MY MIND

The idea that Young couldn't sing is rendered a nonsense by "Out Of My Mind", his second vocal on *Buffalo Springfield*, and a track that rivals Stills' "For What It's Worth" as one of the record's highlights.

A song of ethereal and haunting beauty, like "Flying On The Ground Is Wrong" it deals with the dislocation caused by fame and speaks eloquently of Young's anxieties about the life of a pop star. His concerns were somewhat premature, for the Springfield were hardly superstars at the time and the album that included the song stuck at No. 80 in the *Billboard* chart. "It wasn't happening to them then," Dickie Davis recalls. "The band had the illusion of success but not the reality."

But the lines "All I hear are screams from outside the limousines that are taking me out of my mind" express Young's oddly paradoxical attitude to success. He desired and courted fame with an almost manic obsession and was highly competitive with Stills over who should lead the band. But at the same time, he was deeply fearful of the consequences of fame, creating a basic insecurity and an identity crisis that was to fuel much of his early songwriting.

MR SOUL

Almost as soon as Buffalo Springfield's debut album was released, they began work on a follow-up, which Atco, their record company, wanted to call *Stampede*. Young's capricious decision to quit the group in May 1967 meant that the album never saw the light of day in its originally conceived form. His departure turned out to be temporary, but it caused him to miss the group's performance at the Monterey Pop Festival alongside Otis Redding, Jimi Hendrix and Janis Joplin, among others. Ironically, given their later association, Young's place on stage was taken by David Crosby, who had just been thrown out of the Byrds.

"I couldn't handle it. I don't know why, but something inside of me felt like I wasn't quite on track," is as near as Young has ever got to explaining his decision to quit. "He's a genius, an enigma. Never played a team sport in his life, so he can't make that kind of commitment because he has too many things to do," was Stills' explanation. The rivalry between the two was certainly growing more intense and Springfield bassist Bruce Palmer

NEIL YOUNG: A COMPLEX YOUNG MAN, OBSESSED WITH FAME BUT FEARFUL OF ITS CONSEQUENCES.

was brutally succinct in his verdict. They were, he told Springfield biographer John Einerson, like "two spoiled little brats."

Away from the Springfield, Young began working on a solo project with Jack Nitzsche, who had learned production skills from Phil Spector and had worked with the Rolling Stones. Young was also engaged to produce the classic *Forever Changes* album by the cult LA band Love, but backed out after arranging one song, "The Daily Planet". Instead, with the Springfield's label, Atco, refusing to release him from his contract, by August he was back in the group, contributing three songs to *Buffalo Springfield Again*.

"Mr Soul", which opens the album, was another of Young's observations on the shallowness of fame and his sense of alienation and was written in hospital at the UCLA Medical Center, where he had been taken following an epileptic seizure on stage during a Springfield gig at the Melodyland Theatre, Anaheim, in September 1966.

Based loosely on the riff from the Rolling Stones' "Satisfaction", the song is "respectfully dedicated to the ladies of the Whiskey A Go-Go and the women of Hollywood." The club had go-go dancers in cages. "It was great," Young recalled to Nick Kent 30 years later. "We knew them all. We would look up there and say 'hi' to them. They were right there while we were playing. It was an inspiration."

But Young was disturbed by a darker side to the scene as well: "There were a lot of problems happening with the Springfield. There were a lot of distractions, too. Groupies. Drugs. Then there were all these other people. They were always around, giving you grass, trying to sell you hippie clothes." He admits he became haunted by the feeling that it was a world into which he did not fit, and the lyrics to "Mr Soul" throw some light on why he decided to quit the group.

Recorded in Atlantic's New York studio in an eventful session after a gig at Ondine's in January 1967, the song was also taped against the backdrop of a major fight between the group and its managers and producers, Charlie Greene and Brian Stone. The Springfield evicted the pair from the studio and Stills and Young took over the session. When the album was released, the track's production was credited to "Charlie and Brian with a little help from their friends".

There was also further disagreement over Young's vocal and versions of the song, for which recordings were made with both Stills and Furay taking the lead. In the end, Young got his way. He was so protective towards the song that, according to Springfield drummer Dewey Martin, he even refused to allow Otis Redding to record it as a single. Clearly "Mr Soul" meant a lot to him and the song has remained a live favourite, appearing in both his acoustic and electric sets to this day.

EXPECTING TO FLY

PREPARED TO LET OTHERS SING HIS SONGS ON THE SPRINGFIELD DEBUT, YOUNG BECAME INCREASINGLY INSISTENT ABOUT TAKING THE LEAD.

Young had experimented with a bigger, semi-orchestral sound on "Out Of My Mind" and the approach reached new heights on the multi-layered "Expecting To Fly", which he assembled "from two or three different songs that I moulded together and changed around." Although it appeared on *Buffalo Springfield Again*, the song hardly features the group at all and was a product of Young's brief solo sabbatical, during which he worked with Jack Nitzsche who added the ethereal orchestral score and the stereo phasing. The only other Springfield member to appear on the track was Furay, who added a harmony vocal.

The song has a mysterious and haunting quality, enhanced by Nitzsche's "wall of sound" production, a technique he had learned from his work with Phil Spector. Young later defended "Expecting To Fly" against criticisms that the song's multi-layering in places renders the words inaudible. "They are buried in spots," he admitted. "But the general mood of the song is there. It's based on an old theory. The new style is to try to hear every instrument clearly. The old way of recording is the Phil Spector idea of blending them all so they sound like a wall of sound." The track bombed when released as a single, reaching No. 98 in the Billboard chart.

BROKEN ARROW

The extraordinary sound collage that is "Broken Arrow", which closed the second Springfield album, was Young's most ambitious song to date. Created from fragments of various other songs, including "Down Down Down" (which eventually appeared on the Springfield box set) and two pieces logged in the Atlantic archives as "Ball Park" and "Theme Jazz", "Broken Arrow" clearly owes something to the experimentation of the Beatles' *Sgt Pepper's Lonely Hearts Club Band* and opens with a brief reprise of "Mr Soul" sung by Dewey Martin and the sound of screaming fans, recorded at a 1966 Beatles' concert.

Once again, the lyrical impetus comes from Young's sense of alienation and paranoia, and the song is split into three distinct sections. The first deals with the nature of fame and the relationship between star and fans, the second with growing up and the loss of innocence and the third with a romantic idealism.

The whole piece is tied together with a refrain about an Indian holding a broken arrow. "It's just an image of being very scared and mixed up," Young would explain later. "The broken arrow is the sign of peace, usually after losing a war. A broken arrow usually means that somebody has lost a lot."

In effect, it's a rite-of-passage song, although ten years later Young was able to joke about the song's youthful preoccupations. "I wrote this after quitting the group in '67, due to one of many identity crises," he recalled in the liner note to the *Decade* anthology. "Joined up again soon enough to cut this one though. Took over a hundred takes to get it."

Those multiple takes were the source of some frustration to his fellow band members, who complained that Young kept them in the dark about his vision for the song, teaching them their parts only as required. "We learned it as we recorded it," Stills says.

In the album credits, the song is dedicated to Ken Koblun, an old Canadian friend who had briefly played bass with the Springfield. This has led many to believe that Koblun is the Indian, although given Young's notorious self-absorption at the time, it appears far more probable that he cast himself in the role. The song's importance in his canon cannot be underestimated and he later named his ranch and studio Broken Arrow.

ON THE WAY HOME

UNUSUAL FOR ITS TIME, THE BUFFALO SPRINGFIELD LINE-UP FEATURED THREE ELECTRIC GUITARS.

By the time the third and final Springfield album *Last Time Around* appeared in August 1968, the group had imploded. Typically, Young had been the first to jump ship. The group had been in the studio since late 1967, recording tracks for a third album, but by February the following year, Young had simply ceased showing up. Even before then, he and Stills worked separately in LA's Sunset Sound studios and had ceased even contributing backing vocals to each other's songs.

The final straw in Young's decision to quit was a group drug bust in March 1968: Stills escaped charges by climbing out of a window; Young was less fortunate and used the incident to announce his intention to quit. This time it was for good. The Springfield limped on for a few more weeks to fulfil live dates before disbanding in early May.

"I just couldn't handle it towards the end," Young says. "It wasn't me scheming for a solo career, it wasn't anything but my nerves. Everything started to go too fast. There was a big problem in my head. I just wasn't mature enough to deal with it."

It was left to Furay and new recruit Jim Messina to cobble together the third album that Atco was demanding. *Last Time Around* found Young represented by just two compositions and one collaboration with Furay.

That Young invited Furay to take the vocal on "On The Way Home", which was planned as the Springfield's next single, is an indication of the extent to which he had lost interest in the group. They had begun recording the song at Sunset Sound, LA, on November 14 under the working title "Telephone Pole", a reference to Stills crashing his Ferrari into a pole on the way to the studio that day. Released as the group's final single, "On The Way Home" stalled at No. 82 on the *Billboard* chart.

IT'S SO HARD TO WAIT

Last Time Around also sees Young getting a co-writing credit on "It's So Hard To Wait", a song that began life under the title "Just Can't Seem To Get Movin'". In essence, it's a Furay song with Young's contribution restricted to the lyric of the bridge, "I hope that you care more than a little for me, It's so hard to wait."

"I don't ever remember Neil and I sitting down and collaborating on a song like 'hey, let's write a song together'," Furay says. "But I think he had a fragment and I had a song that fit with it and we put it together."

I AM A CHILD

Young's only other major contribution to the Springfield's farewell album is "I Am A Child". The song, his lone vocal on the album, was in part written as a response to Furay's "A Child's Claim To Fame", which had appeared on *Buffalo Springfield Again* and which was a cynical observation on Young's come-and-go antics. Young clearly did not take offence because he contributed guitar and harmony vocals to Furay's song.

However, Furay was not asked to reciprocate on "I Am A Child", which borrowed the melody from "The Rent Is Always Due", which Young had first recorded in New York in 1965 on his demo for Elektra Records. Young recorded the song in isolation, with only drummer Dewey Martin from the band invited to play on the track. Rather than turn to the disintegrating Springfield camp for musical support, he preferred to recruit the boyfriend of the studio receptionist to play bass.

When *Last Time Around* was released, Young publicly disowned the album. "Such a disgraceful mess that I can't bear to listen to it," he fumed to an American teen magazine. In fact, it was a better record than Young admitted. Even the Springfield's scraps were better than a banquet from most bands. But it was the end of an era. Young's extraordinary solo career, which would still be going strong four decades later, was about to begin.

NEIL YOUNG

Recorded	August to October 1968, Hollywood and San Francisco, California.
Produced by	Neil Young, David Briggs, Jack Nitzsche and Ry Cooder.
Musicians	Neil Young (guitars, piano, synthesizer, harpsichord, pipe organ, vocals) Additional personnel: Ry Cooder (guitar), Jack Nitzsche (electric piano), Jim Messina (bass), Carol Kaye (bass), George Grantham (drums), Earl Palmer (drums), Merry Clayton, Brenda Holloway, Patrice Holloway, Gloria Richetta Jones, Sherlie Matthews, Gracia Nitzsche (backing vocals).

THE EMPEROR OF WYOMING
THE LONER
IF I COULD HAVE HER TONIGHT
I'VE BEEN WAITING FOR YOU
THE OLD LAUGHING LADY
STRING QUARTET FROM WHISKEY BOOT HILL
HERE WE ARE IN THE YEARS
WHAT DID YOU DO
TO MY LIFE
I'VE LOVED HER SO LONG
LAST TRIP TO TULSA

Despite Young's protestations that he had never "schemed" for a solo career, it was clear to anyone connected with Buffalo Springfield that this was where he was headed. Before joining the group, he had worked briefly as a solo performer around the folk clubs and coffee-houses of Ontario, where he had first met Stephen Stills. Then he had attempted to go solo in the summer of 1967, when he briefly left Buffalo Springfield and began working with producer Jack Nitzsche, only for Atco, the group's record company, to refuse to release him from his contract.

The notion of a solo career never went away and during the recording of what was to be the third and final Buffalo Springfield album in early 1968, it was obvious to his fellow band members that Young was holding back several of his best songs for some future project of his own.

After the Springfield disintegrated, Young worked briefly with the Monkees, appearing on two of their songs, "You And I" and "As We Go Along". But this was merely a diversion. On the recommendation of Joni Mitchell, he recruited Elliot Roberts as his manager, who swiftly secured him a solo recording contract with Reprise, Frank Sinatra's record label, and a $20,000 advance. Jack Nitzsche, who had recorded "The Lonely Surfer", one of the label's first hits, had a good relationship with Reprise boss Mo Ostin and helped to broker the deal – even though when Sinatra had set up the label in 1960, he had instructed his executives never to sign any rock'n'roll acts. Roberts has played an enduring part in Young's career and remains his manager to this day.

"I JUST COULDN'T HANDLE IT TOWARDS THE END… IT WASN'T ME SCHEMING FOR A SOLO CAREER."
NEIL YOUNG ON LEAVING BUFFALO SPRINGFIELD.

Sensibly, Young had decided not to fritter away his advance on drugs, groupies and fast living but instead to invest it in property. He also took a conscious decision to move away from the distractions of the Hollywood music scene, leaving his house in Laurel Canyon for the more rural setting of Topanga. It was in a local coffee shop where he met his first wife, Susan Acevado, who already had a seven-year-old daughter and ran the Canyon Kitchen restaurant.

Young spent the late summer of 1968 assembling the team that would work on his first solo record. Nitzsche remained a key player, although he disappeared to work on the soundtrack of the movie *Candy* before the album was finished. Far more important in the long term was David Briggs, a 24-year-old Topanga neighbour who Young had met when the two of them were both scouting the canyon looking for suitable properties to buy. Briggs found a house first and for a time Young slept on his couch. Briggs co-produced the debut album with Young and remained a mainstay of his production team until his death from cancer in 1995.

Among the musicians Young hired was Ry Cooder, the brilliant young slide guitarist who a year later turned down the chance of a berth in the Rolling Stones as Brian Jones's replacement, and who would in the distant future become a world music guru, producing the multi-platinum Cuban album, *Buena Vista Social Club*. Others brought on board included bass player Jim Messina, a late recruit to Buffalo Springfield in its dying days, and drummer George Grantham, both of whom at the time were putting together the pioneering country-rock outfit Poco.

The album, titled simply *Neil Young*, appeared in January 1969. Recorded partly in LA and partly in San Francisco, on its cover was a striking original oil painting of Young by Roland Diehl. The top half of the portrait featured an idyllic rural scene and the bottom half showed a city skyline – an accurate reflection the duality of Young's musical influences on the record.

Commercially the album flopped and failed to dent the charts on either side of the Atlantic. The record has also divided Young's supporters ever since. In his sprawling but masterful biography, *Neil Young – Zero To Sixty*, Johnny Rogan describes it as "one of his greatest achievements" and "among the best five albums he ever recorded." However, Sylvie Simmons, a massive fan who conducted one of the best interviews of Young's later career for *Mojo* magazine, is less impressed. In her excellent and concise monograph, *Reflections In A Broken Glass*, Simmons criticizes the album as "nowhere near immediate enough," dismisses its production as "turgid" and suggests "a sparer, more intimate sound" would have done the songs greater justice.

Certainly there is no other album quite like it in Young's extensive discography. After his solo debut, he would adopt a raw and earthier approach to recording, working "live" in the studio, with overdubs kept to a minimum. On *Neil Young* he was still in thrall to the Phil Spector/Jack Nitzsche "wall of sound" style, using grandiose, semi-orchestral arrangements and painstaking multi-tracking.

Ultimately, though, Young was not happy with the results, and his dissatisfaction was partly responsible for his abandonment of the style in favour of a more spontaneous approach. He complained bitterly that his vocals had been ruined during mastering (a criticism he made publicly at the time and which can have done nothing to bolster the record's meagre sales) and later forced Reprise to issue a second remastered version, which he considered a radical improvement.

HEADING FOR THE COUNTRY – YOUNG INVESTED HIS BUFFALO SPRINGFIELD EARNINGS IN A PROPERTY IN RURAL CALIFORNIA.

In truth, the differences between the two editions are not huge. The remixed version has a marginally enhanced clarity, particularly around some of the guitar work. But Young's vocals remain buried deep in the album's densely multi-tracked backdrop – just as they had done on Buffalo Springfield's "Expecting To Fly", which he had also recorded with Nitzsche and which he had defended against the same kinds of criticism.

He blamed Reprise for the album's technical faults, although his complaints might have been better directed a little closer to home, for the swamping of his voice was mostly his own doing. His old insecurities about his singing had not gone away and he later admitted, "I was paranoid about my voice, so on my first LP I buried my voice intentionally."

Whatever the failings of the album's production, few have ever questioned the quality of the songs themselves – intensely personal, compellingly atmospheric and deeply cinematic in their imagery. Decades later, at least two of them, "The Loner" and "The Old Laughing Lady", continued to turn up in Young's live sets.

THE EMPEROR OF WYOMING

With a perversity that would soon come to be recognized as typical, Young chose to open one of the most enduring solo careers in modern music in anonymous fashion with a throw-away, two-minute, string-laden, country-tinged instrumental in an old-fashioned waltz tempo. A pleasant but insubstantial tune, "The Emperor of Wyoming" never really gets going and sounds like a fragment that he never quite got around to working up into a proper song. You keep waiting for the vocal to come in but, of course, it never does. It's all part of the joke, and for most of his career, Young's humour has tended to be overlooked. As David Briggs once remarked, "You analyse his songs and everybody thinks here's this melancholy guy, this tortured, inner-looking person. But from the first minute I knew him, I saw him as a prankster and a joker."

"I WAS PARANOID ABOUT MY VOICE, SO ON THE FIRST LP I BURIED MY VOICE INTENTIONALLY."
NEIL YOUNG

THE LONER

It was immediately assumed by many on the record's release that Young had written "The Loner" about Stephen Stills. The notion that his old Buffalo Springfield sparring partner was "the perfect stranger, like a cross of himself and a fox" gained further credence when Stills himself covered the track on his 1976 album, *Illegal Stills*. Yet Young's own notorious self-absorption surely would indicate that his own personality was far more likely to be the song's true subject matter. After all, it was Young, not Stills, who had experienced the most difficulties in Buffalo Springfield with the concept of playing as a member of a team, and who was later described by the Springfield's bass player Bruce Palmer as a "cold-hearted, self-righteous son of a bitch who doesn't give a damn about anybody other than himself."

Whatever the true identity of "The Loner", the song has a superbly balanced inner tension. Written during the last days of Buffalo Springfield, it was the first track Young recorded with David Briggs as producer and JIm Messina and George Grantham as the rhythm section, both of whom went uncredited on the record sleeve. It is also a notable example of Young's uncertainties about his own voice – the lead vocal being unusually low in the mix.

Young would later go on to write other songs that were more clearly about Stills – notably "Stringman" and "Cocaine Eyes." Of the two, Stills must surely be more comfortable with the former. "Cocaine Eyes" throws a stark spotlight on the price paid for rock star drug indulgence and appeared on the 1989 album *Eldorado*, released only in Japan. "Stringman" was written in 1976 when the two were working together in the Stills-Young Band and contains the heartfelt line, "There is no dearer friend of mine that I know in this life." It eventually surfaced on the 1993 live recording *Unplugged*.

IF I COULD HAVE HER TONIGHT

Chiming guitars that sound as if they might have come straight from the Byrds' 1967 album *Notorious Byrd Brothers* introduce a beautiful melody and a simple heart-on-sleeve tale of falling in love. With a lyric filled with yearning and uncertainty, "If I Could Have Her Tonight" is an under-appreciated and neglected gem in Young's canon that he hasn't seen fit to revive in concert since. At only just over two minutes long it has an incomplete feel and fades out in a way that suggests Young never got around to writing a proper ending.

I'VE BEEN WAITING FOR YOU

PORTRAIT OF THE ARTIST – NEIL YOUNG CAPTURED DEEP IN THOUGHT.

Young wrote "I've Been Waiting For You" after meeting his first wife, Susan Acevado. "I've been looking for a woman to save my life, Not to beg or to borrow, A woman with the feeling of losing once or twice," he sings with suitable yearning. Susan Acevado certainly fitted the bill and was not one of the teenage girls who hung around the Springfield at the Whisky A Go-Go to whom Young had dedicated "Mr Soul". When Young first met her she already had a seven-year-old daughter, Tia. They married on December 7, 1968, a month before the release of *Neil Young*. (Under the name Susan Young, she later received a credit on *After The Gold Rush* – feminists might think somewhat patronizingly – for sewing the patches on her husband's jeans. The days of women's lib were clearly still some way off.)

The song was heavily overdubbed and Young described the process to *Rolling Stone* in 1970. "When I put on the lead guitar I was really into it that day... in the beginning we put down the acoustic guitar and bass and drums, that's the smallest track I ever did... then we dropped the acoustic guitar because it didn't really fit with the other things that I put on... the pipe organ was put on... the vocal was done in a different studio... it does stick together, though."

THE OLD LAUGHING LADY

"The Old Laughing Lady" first appeared in demo form around the time of *Buffalo Springfield Again,* but was not seriously considered for the album. It then cropped up again on a tentative running list of songs for the third Springfield album in January 1968, when it was – presumably in error – credited to both Young and Stills.

"Jack Nitzsche and I did this one together," Young said of the version that eventually made it on to his debut solo album. "It was a first take overdub vocal for me. Singing in the studio was starting to get easier. It was at this time that Jack told me everything was temporary."

The song builds slowly from an acoustic beginning to a full-on gospel style chorus, courtesy of Gracia Nitzsche, Merry Clayton (who around the same time did a similar job for the Rolling Stones on "Gimme Shelter"), Brenda Holloway, Patricia Holloway, Gloria Richetta Jones and Sherlie Matthews.

The "old laughing lady" is a metaphor for death and both the lyric and the enveloping, trademark Nitzsche production (with assistance from Ry Cooder) conveys a suitably haunting sense of mystery.

STRING QUARTET FROM WHISKEY BOOT HILL

Side two of *Neil Young* also opened with an instrumental. "String Quartet From Whiskey Boot Hill" was arranged and produced by Nitzsche with assistance from Young and Cooder and was derived from a song of the same name that Young had first worked on with Nitzsche in May 1967. The title also reappeared as part of the medley that was "Country Girl" on 1970s' Crosby, Stills, Nash and Young album, *Deja Vu*.

The original song was never realized, but Young was so taken with Nitzsche's string arrangement that he decided it deserved a life of its own.

HERE WE ARE IN THE YEARS

An early ecological song, "Here We Are In The Years" started life as the Buffalo Springfield instrumental "Falcon Lake (Ash On The Floor)", named after a popular resort outside Winnipeg, where Young had taken vacations in his youth and had met one of his first girlfriends. "It was a memory of that time at Falcon Lake. It had Stephen Stills and me and Buddy Miles on drums but we never finished it," Young recalls of the original, which eventually surfaced in 2001 on the Buffalo Springfield box set.

The memory Young refers to survives in the idyllic holiday atmosphere described in the opening line of the reworked version. The song's vision then grows darker as the holiday-makers laugh at the local farmers and – reflecting the painting on the cover – the concrete jungle of the city is contrasted with the tranquillity of the countryside.

"I was trying to say something without going on a pollution and conservation kick. I really don't want to dedicate myself to any cause because it's so limiting," Young later said. He succeeds admirably – the song never descends to the level of propaganda and delivers its message with considerable subtlety, enhanced by a compelling melody.

"NEIL WANTED TO BE BOB DYLAN. I WANTED TO BE THE BEATLES."
STEPHEN STILLS

WHAT DID YOU DO TO MY LIFE

The self-centred examination of a broken love-affair that is "What Did You Do To My Life" finds Young feeling sorry for himself. Worse, by the end, he's in danger of toppling over into self-pity as he whines, "It isn't fair that I should wake up at dawn and not find you there." There's an appealing fragility to the melody, but the vocal is weak and the song is ultimately insubstantial. Unsurprisingly, it has not been revived since.

I'VE LOVED HER SO LONG

The album's final Jack Nitzsche production, "I've Loved Her So Long" is another love song written in the veiled style Young favoured at the time. "She's a victim of her senses, do you know her?" he asks in the opening line. He never names "her" and appears to be singing about a type as much as about a specific individual. Heavily overdubbed in the Spector style, the song is given a heightened sense of drama and an infusion of soul by the same six-strong female chorus who graced "The Old Laughing Lady".

LAST TRIP TO TULSA

Another left-over from Young's Buffalo Springfield days, "Last Trip To Tulsa" was debuted live by the group at a concert in Hollywood in March 1968, on a bill that also featured Jefferson Airplane, Quicksilver Messenger Service and a number of other West Coast groups. The song was originally a contender for inclusion on *Last Time Around*, but was withdrawn once Young had decided to leave the band.

A surreal tale that meanders over nine-and-a-half minutes, the acoustic version of "Last Trip To Tulsa" that was eventually included on *Neil Young* harks back musically not so much to his Springfield rock'n'roll days but to an earlier period when he was attempting to be a solo folk-singer. In the mid-1960s, Bob Dylan reigned supreme as the role model for all aspiring troubadours and Young was no exception, including Dylan songs such as "Just Like Tom Thumb's Blues" in his repertoire. "Neil wanted to be Bob Dylan. I wanted to be the Beatles," Stills recalls of their earliest meeting in 1965.

"The Last Trip To Tulsa" is full of striking but often confused imagery, much in the style of Dylan's epic "Desolation Row" but lacking that song's internal coherence. The scatter-gun lyrics range over a number of weighty subjects including religion, gender confusion and an apocalyptic vision of the long-feared Californian earthquake ("the West Coast is falling, I see rocks in the sky"), but cloaked in a deliberate obscurantism. On first hearing, the song creates an illusion of profundity. Closer inspection suggests that much of it is merely absurd. At best today it sounds like an intriguing period piece and Young himself soon dismissed the song. "After the album came out that's the one I really didn't like," he admitted to *Rolling Stone* in 1970. "It sounds overdone. It just sounds like a mistake to me."

EVERYBODY KNOWS THIS IS NOWHERE

Recorded	January and March 1969, Hollywood, California.
Produced by	Neil Young, David Briggs.
Musicians	Neil Young (guitar, vocals) Crazy Horse: Danny Whitten (guitar, vocals), Billy Talbot (bass), Ralph Molina (drums, vocals) Additional personnel: Robin Lane (guitar, vocals, Bobby Notkoff (violin).

CINNAMON GIRL
EVERYBODY KNOWS THIS IS NOWHERE
(WHEN YOU'RE ON) THE LOSING END
ROUND AND ROUND (IT WON'T BE LONG)
DOWN BY THE RIVER
RUNNING DRY (REQUIEM FOR THE ROCKETS)
COWGIRL IN THE SAND

Dissatisfied with the sound on *Neil Young* and bored and exhausted by the long hours in the studio that its multi-layered and endlessly over-dubbed style entailed, Young was determined to pursue a more immediate and visceral approach on his second solo album. At first he had little idea how to go about it, until he turned to a group called the Rockets that he had encountered playing the clubs of Los Angeles.

"THE CRAZY HORSE SOUND CAME FROM ALL FOUR OF US. I DON'T THINK NEIL WOULD HAVE FOUND THAT SOUND WITH ANYONE ELSE."
RALPH MOLINA

Young had first met two of the band's members, Billy Talbot and Danny Whitten, in the fall of 1966. The introductions were made either by a girl called Autumn or by Whitten's girlfriend, Robin Lane – the details have grown clouded over time. But they were all near neighbours in Laurel Canyon and Young became particularly close to Whitten, whose ambitions as a songwriter he encouraged. Whitten, in turn, was a fan of Young's voice (which not many were at the time), and helped him get over his insecurities as a singer.

The Rockets, who released their own debut album on the White Whale label in early 1968, and Young began spending more time with them. On at least one occasion – and much to the chagrin of Stephen Stills – he even missed a Buffalo Springfield recording session in favour of an informal jam with his new friends at Talbot's house. By the summer, he had quit the Springfield for good and when the Rockets secured the most important booking of their career at the Whisky A Go Go – legendary club venue on West Hollywood's Sunset Strip and the scene of some of Buffalo Springfield's earliest triumphs – Young happily accepted an invitation to sit in with them.

To his delight he found The Rockets rocked considerably harder than the Springfield ever had – or than he and Jack Nitzsche had managed on *Neil Young*, which he had just finished recording. Inspired by the experience, he promptly suggested they should become his backing band. He initially suggested the name Neil Young and the War Babies, with the intention that The Rockets should continue as a separate entity in their own right. In reality, this never happened. Once they began recording with Young, the group's violinist Bobby Notkoff found his role was limited and dropped out, leaving a nucleus of Whitten on guitar, Talbot on bass and Ralph Molina on drums. The Rockets ceased to exist and the War Babies name was also thrown out.

"That's when it evolved into Crazy Horse. It just happened." This was how Molina would later describe the event to Johnny Rogan, the most thorough of Young's numerous biographers. "The Crazy Horse sound came from all four of us. I don't think Neil would have found that sound with

anyone else. We were all feel players and that was the way we played – with raw emotion."

Young agreed. He told friends that the first time he heard the Rockets they struck him as "an American Rolling Stones." The comment was significant, for many had referred to Buffalo Springfield as "the American Beatles". Now Young was after a grittier, dirtier sound that was to take his guitar-playing and vocal style to new and previously unimagined places. "Crazy Horse is a very soulful feeling for me," he explained many years later. "They give me a support that no one else can give me, they afford me the possibilities of doing more with my guitar and my voice and feeling than anybody else."

The meeting with The Rockets and that revelatory date together at the Whisky A Go-Go meant that within weeks of the release of his debut solo album, Young was steering a completely new course. By mid-February he was on tour with Crazy Horse, playing residencies at The Bitter End in New York and the Troubadour in LA and the group helped him to define the electric sound that was to become his trademark.

Young also wrote a series of new songs with Crazy Horse in the back of his mind (several of them in bed during a bout of flu), and within a fortnight they were in the studio. Despite the many twists and turns of Young's long career and a major tragedy within the group (see the chapter on Tonight's The Night), Crazy Horse have remained loyal acolytes and were still playing with their mentor more than 30 years later. In all that time, it is doubtful whether they have bettered the extraordinary *Everybody Knows This Is Nowhere*, still regarded by many as one of the defining albums of modern rock'n'roll.

Released in a grainy cover that depicts Young as some kind of mountain man in a checked lumberjack shirt, the album's spontaneity and immediacy were in stark contrast to the painstaking way he had previously worked. Remarkably, the record was in the stores in May 1969, just four months after the release of *Neil Young*, and it created a creative template that dictated how he attempted to record for the rest of his career.

CINNAMON GIRL

NEIL YOUNG: A MAN IN SEARCH OF A NEW SOUND.

In early 1969, just as his association with the Rockets/Crazy Horse was coming to life, Young took to his bed in his Topanga house with a debilitating dose of flu. With his mind in an altered state due to a fever that

he claimed rolled up to 103 degrees, he wrote three songs, including "Cinnamon Girl".

All three songs were composed on an acoustic guitar, but excited by the possibilities of working with Danny Whitten and his friends, Young wanted to try them out with electric instrumentation and a backbeat. "Cinnamon Girl" was the first song he recorded with Crazy Horse in the studio and the result is a euphoric marriage of hard-rocking riffs and sweet melody. The dreamy, wistful lyrics reflect his feverish state and the mysterious effect is only enhanced by his later hand-scribbled non-explanation, "Wrote this for a city girl on peeling pavement coming at me through Phil Ochs' eyes playing finger cymbals. It was hard to explain to my wife."

8901 SUNSET BOULEVARD – BETTER KNOWN AS THE LEGENDARY WHISKY A GO GO.

The song helped to establish Neil Young as a unique lead guitar stylist, combining feedback, distortion, one-note solos and clever use of vibrato and sustain, although the effect was based more on intuition and feel than possessing a particularly skilled fretboard technique. Indeed, many years later, *Rolling Stone* magazine would describe Young as "an abstract expressionist of the guitar."

The glory of "Cinnamon Girl" is enhanced by the open guitar tuning in which it was written, something which Young had first used when playing on Stills' composition "Bluebird" on *Buffalo Springfield Again*. "We discovered this D modal tuning around the same time in 1966," he told Nick Kent. "That was when ragas were happening and D modal made it possible to have that droning sound going all the time. That's where it started, only I took it to the next level, which is how 'The Loner' and 'Cinnamon Girl' happened."

Released as a single, the song made No. 55 in the Billboard charts and has remained a mainstay of his live shows. In-concert versions appear on 1979's *Live Rust* and again on 1991's *Arc/Weld*. On both he is accompanied by the ever-faithful Crazy Horse.

EVERYBODY KNOWS THIS IS NOWHERE

The title track of Young's second solo effort had originally been recorded for the *Neil Young* album, although rendered in a radically different arrangement with woodwind accompaniment, courtesy of Jack Nitzsche. Why Young ultimately held the song back is unclear, but he completely re-recorded it for his second album, this time with twanging country-style guitar and suitably ragged backing harmonies by Danny Whitten and Crazy Horse. The lyric with its heartfelt complaint about the author's need to "get away from this day to day running around" and to "go back home and take it easy" was born of his disillusionment with the Hollywood music scene, which had caused his move to Topanga following the break-up of Buffalo Springfield.

An earlier version of the song without Crazy Horse appeared on promotional pressings of a US single in March 1969 and Young revived the song on his 1982 European tour with the Trans-Band, which found him reunited with the Springfield's original bassist, Bruce Palmer.

ROUND AND ROUND (IT WON'T BE LONG)

"Round and Round (It Won't Be Long)" had been around since Buffalo Springfield days, when Young went into Gold Star studios in August 1967 and recorded a solo demo, listed in the Atlantic archive as "Round and Round and Round". Demos of several other songs, including "The Old Laughing Lady", were recorded on the same day.

The original demo eventually appeared on the Buffalo Springfield box set and the version Young re-recorded 18 months later remained largely true to the original arrangement. Yet atmospherically it is very different, slowed down and given an ethereal quality by the haunting voice of Robin Lane on the chorus. Lane, the daughter of Dean Martin's pianist Kenny Lane, had been Danny Whitten's girlfriend, but was romantically involved with Young before he met and married Susan Acevado. Although she was never a member of the Rockets, she had been a participant in the late night jam sessions at Talbot's house in Laurel Canyon that Young had attended when he was extricating himself from Buffalo Springfield.

The only other musician on the track is Whitten, which given Lane's relationships with both men, creates an intriguing *ménage à trois*. Round and round, indeed. Young later described the track as "one of my favourites" before offering a rambling explanation of how the echo from the guitars and the voices switched channels because of the way the trio were rocking back and forth in front of the microphones. "Those things are not featured. They're just in it," he explained obliquely.

According to the usually reliable Johnny Rogan, the lyrics are "clearly influenced by the Bokanist song in Kurt Vonnegut's *Cat's Cradle*." We shall have to take his word. The novel is full of fragments of songs and calypsos by Vonnegut's fictional character, Bokonon, but this author's researches failed to reveal any obvious similarities to Young's lyric.

DOWN BY THE RIVER

The nine-minute track that closes side one of *Everybody Knows This Is Nowhere* remains one of the greatest monuments in Young's canon. "Down By The River" was written when Young had a fever, on the same day as

CRAZY HORSE PROVIDED NEIL YOUNG WITH THE GRITTY NEW SOUND HE HAD BEEN AFTER.

"Cinnamon Girl" and "Cowgirl In The Sand" – "lying in bed sweating with scraps of paper covering the bed," he later recalled

Recorded when Crazy Horse had been together just two weeks, it's a controlled but inspired jam, with Young ripping notes out of his electric guitar, which then splinter and shatter with an intense brutality. "A lot of people think we play simple and there is no finesse," Young later said of his jams with Crazy Horse. "But we're not trying to impress anybody, we just want to play with the feeling. It's like a trance we get into." "Down By The River" is the perfect manifestation of the trance-like musical possession of which the group at its intuitive best was capable.

According to Crazy Horse drummer Ralph Molina, Young copied the chord sequence for "Down By The River" from a Danny Whitten composition called "Music On The Road", although as the song was never recorded there is no way of verifying this. Whitten, who plays on the track, does not receive a writing credit, so the story appears improbable. The origins of the song's dramatic narrative and its refrain of "I shot my baby" are similarly obscure. "No, there's no real murder in it. It's about blowing your thing with a chick," Young told Robert Greenfield in 1970. "It's a plea, a desperate cry."

However, at a concert in New Orleans in 1984, he told a different story. In a lengthy preamble to the song, he claimed it was about "a guy who had a lot of trouble controlling himself". He continued to paraphrase the lyrics, describing a very literal meeting by a river in which the man tells the woman she's cheated on him once too often. "He reached down into his pocket and pulled a little revolver out and he said, 'Honey I hate to do this, but you've pushed me too far!'"

Whatever the truth of the matter, the song exudes a dark passion and a simmering tension that have ensured it has remained a concert favourite ever since and a highlight of numerous CSNY shows where it became the vehicle for some epic guitar duels between Young and Stills.

(WHEN YOU'RE ON) THE LOSING END

The slightest of the seven songs on *Everybody Knows This Is Nowhere*, "(When You're On) The Losing End" is an enjoyable country waltz with a downbeat lyric and a vocal that at times sounds like a deliberate pastiche of the Nashville style. Somewhat surprisingly, the song was revisited five years later on Crosby, Stills, Nash and Young's 1974 reunion stadium tour.

RUNNING DRY (REQUIEM FOR THE ROCKETS)

Young's arrival on the scene had effectively finished the Rockets as a band in their own right, and although Crazy Horse opened exciting new doors for several members of the group, it had marked the end of the road for violinist Bobby Notkoff. Fittingly then, Young employed him to add some keening, melancholic fiddle to "Running Dry", the song he dedicated to the group's memory. It was the only time Young and Notkoff would record together and, if not unique, the subtle interplay between guitar and violin is highly unusual. The only similarly effective combination that comes to mind is the teaming of Richard Thompson and Dave Swarbrick on Fairport Convention's 1970 folk-rock classic, *Liege and Lief*.

Lyrically the song works on several different levels. Taken literally, it can be interpreted as a routine tale of romantic betrayal with lines such as "I left my love with ribbons on and water in her eyes," before Young apologizes, "I'm sorry for the things I've done." The sub-title – "Requiem For The Rockets" – however, adds another altogether more poignant layer of meaning.

"WE'RE NOT TRYING TO IMPRESS ANYBODY, WE JUST WANT TO PLAY WITH FEELING."
NEIL YOUNG

COWGIRL IN THE SAND

Just as side one of *Everybody Knows This Is Nowhere* closes with "Down By The River", side two concluded with the epic guitar pyrotechnics of the even longer "Cowgirl In The Sand". The third of the songs written in a single day when sick in bed with a fever, Young proved its adaptability with a stunning acoustic version a year later on Crosby, Stills, Nash and Young's live album *Four Way Street*.

Lyrically, the song is obscure and dreamlike, addressed to some idealized woman with intriguing references to "sin" and "rust", the latter of which was to become something of a leitmotif in Young's later work. In a performance at London's Festival Hall in 1971, which is widely available on bootleg, he added to the ambiguity by introducing the song as being about "beaches in Spain", even though he admitted at the time he had never visited the country.

Despite the song's successful acoustic incarnation, it is not for its lyrics but as a vehicle for some of the most powerful and untamed lead guitar playing ever recorded that the ten-minute "Cowgirl In The Sand" is perhaps most memorable.

Young himself remains fondly attached the song: it was still in service as a guitar epic more than three decades later, when he released an explosive 18-minute version captured in concert in San Diego in 2000 for the album *Road Rock*.

AFTER THE GOLD RUSH

Recorded	August 1969 to June 1970, Topanga and Hollywood, California.
Produced by	Neil Young, David Briggs, Kendall Pacios.
Musicians	Neil Young (vocals, guitar, piano, harmonica, vibes), Crazy Horse: Danny Whitten (guitar, vocals), Billy Talbot (bass), Ralph Molina (drums, vocals) Additional personnel: Nils Lofgren (guitar, piano, keyboards, vocals), Jack Nitzsche (piano), Bill Peterson (flugelhorn), Greg Reeves (bass), Stephen Stills (vocals).

TELL ME WHY
AFTER THE GOLD RUSH
ONLY LOVE CAN BREAK YOUR HEART
SOUTHERN MAN
TILL THE MORNING COMES
OH LONESOME ME
DON'T LET IT BRING YOU DOWN
BIRDS
WHEN YOU DANCE I CAN REALLY LOVE
I BELIEVE IN YOU
CRIPPLE CREEK FERRY

BY 1970 YOUNG WAS ENJOYING SUCCESS BOTH AS A SOLO ARTIST AND AS PART OF HIS "SUPERGROUP" COLLABORATION WITH DAVID CROSBY, STEPHEN STILLS AND GRAHAM NASH.

By the release of his third solo album, Young's career had been sent into the stratosphere by his membership of the so-called "supergroup", Crosby, Stills, Nash & Young.

Stephen Stills had begun the process of wooing Young when, in the spring of 1969, he dropped by a Crazy Horse gig at Hollywood's Troubadour and jammed with the band and his old Buffalo Springfield colleague. Together with David Crosby, once of the Byrds and Graham Nash from the British pop group the Hollies, he had already recorded the album *Crosby, Stills and Nash* and it was obvious the group was going to be huge. Yet Stills felt there was a missing element, particularly when CSN came to tour. Several other names had been approached, including Stevie Winwood and Eric Clapton. Both declined. Then Ahmet Ertegun, head of Atlantic Records, suggested Stills should forget old rivalries and approach Young.

Young was at first non-committal. "It took a while. We had to settle whether my name would be included in the billing and what size it would be. I already had a good solo career going," Young recalled to Johnny Rogan. "It took about a month to decide. The music was so good, I just wanted to join in."

Once he'd committed himself, CSNY took to the road, playing both the Woodstock and Altamont festivals. A European tour followed in early 1970 but, as soon as it was over, Young was back in Topanga playing with Crazy Horse again, this time with the addition of his old friend Jack Nitzsche back in the saddle on keyboards.

Although he was undoubtedly excited by the success of CSNY, he remained strangely aloof from his three colleagues and did not attempt to hide the fact that his solo work remained more important to him. It's hard not to agree with Graham Nash who has publicly suggested that Young's decision to join forces with CSN was motivated by the boost he knew it would give his own career.

Even as CSNY's album *Déjà Vu* was topping the album charts in the spring of 1970, Young was far more concerned with putting together *After The Gold Rush*, his third solo album, which was released in September that year. The record created him a new image as a romantic troubadour, and Young found himself linked with such names as James Taylor, Joni Mitchell and Carole King in the vanguard of the army of sensitive singer-songwriters – often referred to in Britain as "the bedsit brigade" – who were to dominate the musical scene in the early 1970s. The romantic mood of the album was further enhanced by the aching fragility of his falsetto voice, which is used to brilliant effect on several of the songs.

"THE MUSIC WAS SO GOOD I JUST WANTED TO JOIN IN."
NEIL YOUNG DISCUSSES CSNY

However, the album that became *After The Gold Rush* had not started out that way. Young's initial plan had been to record a gritty rock album with Crazy Horse. Several tracks were recorded, before Young lost patience with Danny Whitten, who by then was developing an out-of-control drug habit. As Whitten grew increasingly unreliable, an exasperated Young shelved the sessions and dismissed Crazy Horse.

In their place he recruited bassist Greg Reeves, who had been playing with CSNY, and 18-year-old Nils Lofgren, who had first introduced himself backstage at a Crazy Horse gig in Washington in 1969. Lofgren, who had his own band called Grin, had played Young several of his songs and impressed him with his youthful enthusiasm.

When contacted in March 1970 and invited to work on *After The Gold Rush*, Lofgren moved into David Briggs's Topanga home, as Young himself had done two years earlier. For a drummer, Young turned to Crazy Horse's Ralph Molina. Then he solved the problem of where to record by hiring a mixing desk and transporting it to his Topanga home where he had already begun constructing a studio in which he "put the wood on the walls myself," as he later boasted.

There he began recording an entirely new set of material, rescuing little from the aborted Crazy Horse sessions. According to Lofgren, he wrote four of the new songs in six days and the entire album was recorded inside a week.

TELL ME WHY

Despite his lack of experience, Lofgren fitted readily into the role previously filled by Whitten of Young's right-hand man and foil, and his presence on both harmony and guitar is strong on the album's opening song. But the sweet and gentle melodic feel of "Tell Me Why" also suggests the influence of Crosby, Stills and Nash in absentia. In particular, the discipline of singing within the framework of their tight harmonies appears to have banished any lingering self-doubt about his abilities as a vocalist. From its opening lines about sailing "heart ships" through "broken harbours", the song also establishes the romantic singer-songwriter mood that dominates the album.

There's a jaunty innocence in the line "I am lonely but you can free me, all in the way that you smile", although there then comes a barb in the chorus, in which Young questions, "Was it hard to make arrangements with yourself, when you're old enough to repay but young enough to sell?" Presumably the words had some veiled but specific reference to his own life, for he soon stopped performing the song, claiming it was "too intense" for him to sing. Certainly, his marriage to Susan Acevado was already under strain when they started recording *After The Gold Rush*. Young told an interviewer that she had at one point thrown a cup of coffee over him while he was recording the album and by the end of 1970, the couple had separated. Years later in a VH1 documentary, Young admitted, "She was older than I was, and I really wasn't grown up enough for her. It took me a long time to grow up because all my growing up time was spent on music."

AFTER THE GOLD RUSH

"Most of these songs were inspired by the Dean Stockwell/Herb Berman screenplay *After The Gold Rush*", Young noted in the liner notes to the album that shared the same name. The connection of the songs to the script, however, was a loose one. Stockwell was an actor and neighbour who had written a script for a disaster movie in which Topanga had been flooded by a tidal wave following a Californian earthquake. The plot followed the disaster's effect on a number of residents, including a local folk singer. Young loved the script and hoped to appear in the movie. In the end, it failed to get financial backing and was never made. "Too much of an art project," Young later suggested.

The song "After The Gold Rush", performed solo by Young at the piano with a plaintive, high-register vocal, has some relationship to the movie with its apocalyptic visions of ecological catastrophe ("look at mother nature on the run in the 1970s"). But then it takes off into the realms of a science fiction dream, in which extra-terrestrials in silver spaceships save life on earth by carrying "mother nature's silver seed" to a new home beyond the doomed planet. According to producer David Briggs, the song was "written on the spot" and took Young precisely half an hour.

Curiously, "After The Gold Rush" would later become a worldwide hit single when covered *a capella* by the British folk group Prelude in 1974. The group re-recorded the song in 1982 and it became a chart hit for a second time.

ONLY LOVE CAN BREAK YOUR HEART

Another composition in romantic troubadour mode, "Only Love Can Break Your Heart" was, in fact, not particularly self-confessional but was written for Graham Nash, who had just split up with Joni Mitchell. This made Young the third songwriter to document the relationship, Nash having written the cloyingly sentimental "Our House" on the Crosby, Stills, Nash and Young album *Déjà Vu* and Mitchell including her composition "Willy" (her nickname for Nash) on *Ladies Of The Canyon*.

Interestingly, the same Mitchell album included "The Circle Game", written for Young in response to one of his early songs, "Sugar Mountain", while Young wrote another, unreleased song about Mitchell called "Sweet Joni", which he played several times in concert during 1972–73. It was also strongly rumoured that "Stupid Girl" on Young's 1975 album *Zuma* was about Mitchell. The chemistry within CSNY not only created some great music. It also kept the show-biz gossip columnists busy with a web of tangled relationships in what, at times, resembled a counter-culture version of a soap opera.

Not to be left out, Stephen Stills later recorded his own version of "Only Love Can Break Your Heart" on the 1984 album *Right By You*. David Crosby and Joni Mitchell, it may be noted, had been lovers before Nash arrived on the scene.

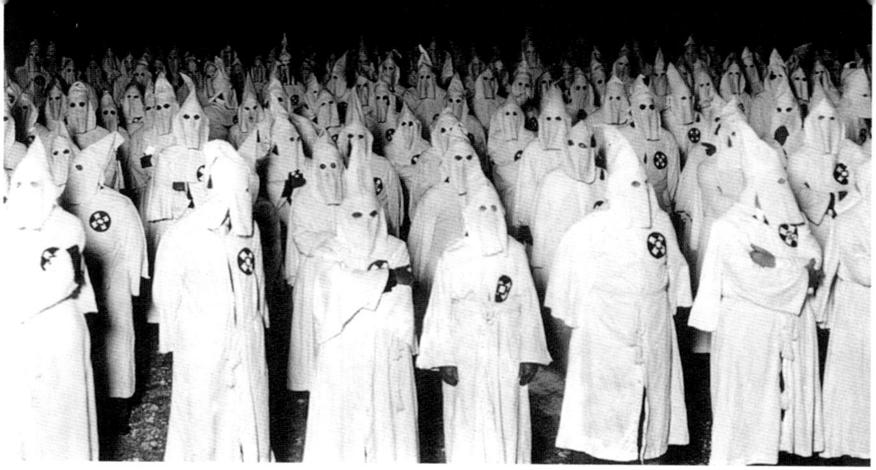

THE KU KLUX KLAN – THE DEEPLY UNATTRACTIVE FACE OF AMERICA'S DEEP SOUTH.

SOUTHERN MAN

A scathing indictment of racism and bigotry, one account of "Southern Man" claims to have its roots in an incident witnessed by Young while the Buffalo Springfield were touring the deep South with the Beach Boys in 1968. Beating up longhairs was at the time regarded as fair sport in certain parts of the South and sitting in a diner one night after a gig with members of the tour retinue, Young overheard a bunch of rednecks plotting to attack them. In the end, an *Easy Rider* scenario was avoided when reinforcements from the touring party arrived giving the hippies numerical supremacy.

Young tells a slightly different story. "This song could have been written on a civil rights march after stopping off to watch *Gone With The Wind*," he joked some years later. Then he went on to claim, "Actually I think I wrote it in the Fillmore East dressing room in 1970."

Certainly CSNY were playing it live by May of that year and an epic version appears on the live album *Four Way Street*. Another live version appeared on 1972's *Journey Thru The Past* but the studio recording has a greater tension than any of the live versions. Indignant and angry, the *After The Gold Rush* version produced not only some of Young's most incendiary guitar playing but one of his best and most anguished vocals. Nightmarish visions of the Ku Klux Klan going about their unspeakable business are evoked as his impassioned voice yells, "I heard screaming and bull whips cracking."

He returned to the theme in "Alabama" on his next album *Harvest*, provoking the southern boogie band Lynyrd Skynyrd to respond with "Sweet Home Alabama", in which they chided, "I hope Neil Young will remember, southern man don't need him around."

TILL THE MORNING COMES

One of the advantages of the old vinyl long-player format was that the opening and closing tracks of the two sides offered four pivotal points around which an album could be structured. Young used them to full advantage and, just as he had opened both sides of *Neil Young* with instrumentals, he chose to close both sides of *After The Gold Rush* with fragments of songs little more than a minute long.

Side one's closer was "Till The Morning Comes", a slight two-line refrain from an unfinished song with a simple piano riff that is lifted briefly by an unexpected (and uncredited) piano solo.

OH LONESOME ME

Don Gibson was a singer and songwriter from North Carolina who had begun recording in the late 1940s and specialized in sentimental but powerful country and western weepies. His compositions included "Sweet Dreams", made famous by Patsy Cline and "I Can't Stop Loving You", which was one of Ray Charles's biggest hits. The B-side of Gibson's own 1958 recording of the latter was "Oh Lonesome Me", which he originally wrote for George Jones.

On the surface it was a strange choice for the first ever cover version Young recorded. Part of the reason for Young's choice may have been less to do with an admiration for Gibson and more to do with his passion for the voice of Roy Orbison, who, in 1967, had recorded an entire album of Gibson's songs. Young's recording predates the rest of *After The Gold Rush* and was the sole survivor from the earlier aborted version of the album. Before he abandoned the recordings, he had told an interviewer he was trying to sound "like Everly Brothers records and Roy Orbison records".

The early recording date – some time in late 1969 – is confirmed by the release of the song as a single in January 1970, some eight months before it appeared on *After The Gold Rush*. Young's voice is maudlin, the harmonica solo unstructured and few of the album's reviewers quite understood why he had included it. "I like it because everybody else seems to hate it so much," Young insisted.

There's an interesting footnote in that on Gibson's original version he actually sings "Ol' lonesome me," but a clerk employed by the song's publishers, Acuff-Rose, mis-transcribed the lyrics.

DON'T LET IT BRING YOU DOWN

Written on CSNY's visit to London in January 1970 when they played the Royal Albert Hall, the lyrics of "Don't Let It Bring You Down" suggest Young had formed a low opinion of Britain on his first professional visit. As a depiction of London's urban decay, the picture he paints appears exaggerated. He may have observed the "old man sitting by the side of the road with the lorries rolling by" of the opening line. But he's surely exaggerating London's blight when he describes a "dead man" lying by the road.

In fact, his vision of a concrete jungle in which the "buildings scrape the sky" and humanity is all but crushed sounds more like New York or Chicago. But Young has seldom been a strictly literal writer, and he presumably set out to paint a universal picture of metropolitan misery.

In a Dutch television film shot the following year, he tried to describe his songwriting style. "The images that I write… I really don't know where they come from," he said. "I just see the pictures in my eyes. Sometimes I can't get them to come but then if I get high or just sit there and wait, all of a sudden it comes." He went on to describe the process as "like having a mental orgasm."

"Don't Let It Bring You Down" has remained a concert favourite and was also included on the live CSNY album *Four Way Street*.

BIRDS

Young first sang "Birds" with the Buffalo Springfield at a Hollywood benefit concert in March 1968 after he had told the band he was quitting. They continued to fulfil live dates, and Richie Furay remembers the group playing "Birds" several times at those last shows. "I thought it was fitting because it was about flying away," he recalls. "Neil played piano on it."

The starkly arresting version recorded for *After The Gold Rush* has Young at the piano playing a series of haunting chords. On one level, the lyric is about the disintegration of a romance, but it can also be interpreted as a direct comment on the demise of the Springfield. Johnny Rogan floats the theory that the "It's over" line is a tribute to Roy Orbison, who had a huge hit song bearing that name, and goes on to dismiss the song as "extremely forced and unconvincing". This seems a harsh judgement and many Young fans regard it as one of his most endearing performances. Certainly, he regarded "Birds" highly himself and made at least three studio recordings of the song. An earlier version from the sessions for the *Neil Young* album later appeared as the B-side to "Only Love Can Break Your Heart" and he also recorded an unreleased version with Crazy Horse in the summer of 1969.

WHEN YOU DANCE I CAN REALLY LOVE

Both Jack Nitzsche and Crazy Horse were back on board for "When You Dance I Can Really Love", one of the last tracks recorded and only the album's second rocker after "Southern Man". Young's anger at Whitten's transgressions had clearly softened and by now it was Nitzsche who was giving him the most grief. According to witnesses, he was obnoxiously drunk much of the time and argued heatedly with Young. Although he attended several sessions, "When You Dance", on which he plays some thumping piano, is the only track he appears on and he took no part in the production process. "Just to get him to play on that song we had to talk him into it," Nils Lofgren recalls.

I BELIEVE IN YOU

Of all the songs on *After The Gold Rush*, "I Believe In You" is the one that most closely fits the confessional singer-songwriter mode. Who it's about and what Young is confessing is another matter. But despite the affirmation of the title, the ballad finds him racked with self-doubt and questioning his own ability to love. Indeed, he sounds so emotionally fragile – even fractured – it would not be hard to imagine James Taylor singing the song.

Young has since offered two explanations of the lyric, neither of which is particularly revelatory. "I think this gets to the heart of the matter," he said obscurely in 1977. "And as Danny Whitten once said, 'I don't want to talk about it.'"

11 years later, talking about it at length to Scott Cohen in *Spin*, he was still casting little light. "What am I talking about? 'Now that you've made

KINGS OF SOUTHERN BOOGIE, LYNYRD SKYNRD WERE NOT IMPRESSED BY NEIL YOUNG'S ATTACKS ON AMERICA'S SOUTHERN STATES.

yourself love me do you think I can change it in a day?' That's a heavy one. That song has the most haunting lyrics. 'Am I lying to you when I say I believe in you?' That's the difference between the song and the poem. The song makes you think of the hook and the hook is 'I believe in you', but the rest of it is in a whole other place."

The song was covered by Rita Coolidge, who had her own place in the CSNY soap opera when Nash stole her away from Stills. The fight over her was chronicled by Crosby in the song "Cowboy Movie", in which Young appears cast as "young Billy".

CRIPPLE CREEK FERRY

After The Gold Rush concludes with a frustrating postscript to what is a great album. Unlike "Till The Morning Comes", the insubstantial two-line throw-away that closed side one, the 90 seconds Young allows us of "Cripple Creek Ferry" are sufficient to suggest a fabulous song in the making. The roots-flavoured melody lurches attractively, not unlike something The Band might have recorded around the same time, and the characters such as the captain and the gambler, who flicker briefly in the intriguingly incomplete lyric, tease us with their untold stories. Sadly, the song was never finished... or if it was, Young has chosen to keep it to himself.

HARVEST

Recorded	January to September 1971, Nashville, Tennessee; Woodside, California; Barking, England.
Produced by	Neil Young, Elliot Mazer, Henry Lewy. Jack Nitzsche.
Musicians	Neil Young and The Stray Gators: Neil Young (vocals, guitar, piano, harmonica), Ben Keith (pedal steel guitar), Jack Nitzsche (piano, slide guitar), Tim Drummond (bass), Kenny Buttrey (drums). Additional personnel: John Harris (piano), Teddy Irwin (guitar), James McMahon (piano), James Taylor (banjo, guitar, backing vocals), David Crosby, Graham Nash, Linda Ronstadt, Stephen Stills (backing vocals).

OUT ON THE WEEKEND
HARVEST
A MAN NEEDS A MAID
HEART OF GOLD
ARE YOU READY FOR THE COUNTRY
OLD MAN
THERE'S A WORLD
ALABAMA
THE NEEDLE AND THE DAMAGE DONE
WORDS (BETWEEN THE LINES OF AGE)

AFTER A CUSTOMS INCIDENT AT HEATHROW AIRPORT, YOUNG WAS FORCED TO MISS THE ISLE OF WIGHT FESTIVAL .

By 1971, when he came to record *Harvest*, Young's life was in a state of turmoil. This was hardly surprising following the events of the previous 12 months. He'd split up with his first wife, Susan, and begun a relationship with the actress Carrie Snodgrass. Then there had been the shock of the Hollywood slayings orchestrated by Charles Manson, whom Young had befriended and even recommended to his record company as a promising singer-songwriter.

He'd moved out of Topanga and bought a ranch at La Honda, which he renamed Broken Arrow. Then, while working on the ranch, he'd damaged his back. The problem was diagnosed as a degenerated spinal disc and required surgery and traction. He'd missed an appearance at the Isle of Wight festival alongside Jimi Hendrix and Joni Mitchell, after customs officers at Heathrow had found "suspicious substances" in his manager Elliott Roberts' luggage and the pair had effectively been deported. When he did get to London in February 1971, he played a triumphant solo show at the Festival Hall and recorded a BBC TV special, but was thrown out of his rented apartment for making too much noise.

Now an international superstar, far bigger than he could ever have imagined in his Buffalo Springfield days, within the space of a few months he had enjoyed chart-topping albums as part of CSNY with *Déjà Vu* and *Four Way Street* and his own top ten platinum album in *After The Gold Rush*. Yet fame brought with it its own burdens. His relations with Crosby, Stills and Nash were strained and he was still not fully reconciled with Crazy Horse, following guitarist Danny Whitten's slide into drug addiction.

Yet out of these chaotic events, Young fashioned the most successful album of his entire career – the chart-topping *Harvest*. He did so by turning, as Bob Dylan had done before him, to a bunch of Nashville session players, whom he renamed the Stray Gators. He made his first trip to Nashville's Quadrafonic studios in February 1971, although it was another 12 months before *Harvest* was released.

As was now his way, Young wrote and recorded rapidly and had enough material for two or three albums. The delay was caused partly by a stay in an LA hospital in August 1971 for an operation on his back and was then extended by a row with his record company over the album's sleeve after Young had objected to his picture appearing on the cover.

He got his way, of course. When *Harvest* was released it came in a plain, wheat-coloured cover printed on high-quality art paper and adorned only with the title and the name of the artist in an old-fashioned script that made it look more like a Victorian hymnal than a rock'n'roll album. The effect was simple but striking and perfectly reflected *Harvest*'s bucolic mood. It also suggested that Young was far smarter than the highly-paid record company executives at Reprise when it came to marketing strategies. As a concession to his record company's wishes, a picture of the artist was included inside – a hopelessly blurred image that could have been almost anyone, photographed in the reflection of a brass door handle.

OUT ON THE WEEKEND

The idea of recording in Nashville came out of a visit Young made to the capital of country in February 1970 to appear on a Johnny Cash television show, recorded at the Ryman Auditorium, the home of the world-famous Grand Ole Opry. After the show, Young went to a party thrown by record

THE RYMAN AUDITORIUM, NASHVILLE, TENNESSEE – HISTORIC HOME TO THE GRAND OLE OPRY.

producer Elliott Mazer, who was an old friend of his own manager, Elliott Roberts. Mazer had worked with Linda Ronstadt, Janis Joplin and Young's fellow Canadian Gordon Lightfoot among others. But he was most impressed by the fact that Mazer had produced an album by the band Area Code 615.Taking its name from the Nashville telephone code, it comprised a bunch of top session musicians, several of whom had played on Dylan's *Nashville Skyline* and whose "Stone Fox Chase" had been adopted as the theme tune by BBC Television's late-night rock show *The Old Grey Whistle Test*.

Mazer, who owned Quadrafonic studios, volunteered to round up a band. In the event, from Area Code 615 he was only able to get drummer Kenny Buttrey, who had also played on *Nashville Skyline*. However, he suggested Ben Keith on pedal steel and Tim Drummond on bass and they went straight into the studio that weekend to begin recording. Under the name the Stray Gators, this core was to become the mainstay of the album.

With Young on acoustic guitar and harmonica, the Gators' trademark down-home sound dominates the opening track. "Out On The Weekend" was not recorded that first weekend, but Young continued to return to Nashville until the album was finished. He liked Mazer, who co-produced most of the album, and loved the ambience of Quadrafonic, which was actually an old house with the original fireplace still in the room where they recorded.

As so often is the case with Young, the song has an emotional ambivalence. On the one hand, there's a woman "so fine she's in my mind" and the comforting image of "her big brass bed". But then there's "the lonely boy" who's "so down today" and "can't relate to joy".

Young himself seemed puzzled by the song's psychology. "I guess my outlook is bleak or desolate or something," he said on the album's release. "Even when I'm happy it sounds like I'm not and when I try to say I'm happy I try to disguise it." He went on to explain that the melancholic-sounding second verse with the lines, "can't relate to joy, he tries to speak and can't begin to say" was meant to be an expression of supreme happiness. "That just means that I'm so happy that I can't get it all out. But it doesn't sound happy. The way I wrote it sounds sad, like I tried to hide it."

HARVEST

The album's title track again features the Stray Gators, this time augmented by John Harris on piano, who create a somewhat plodding country waltz behind Young's plaintive vocal.

Once more, the lyrics reflect Young's apparent psychological inability to accept happiness at face value. Lyrics such as "dream up, dream up, let me fill your cup" are redolent of the fecundity suggested in the song's title. But that's far too simple for the angst-ridden Young. "Will I see you give more than I can take? Will I only harvest some?" he tortures himself, full of gnawing self-doubt.

But the song clearly meant a lot to him. Written in London in February 1971, "Harvest" was premiered the very next day at the Festival Hall, when Young announced that it would be the title song of his next album.

A MAN NEEDS A MAID

While laid-up with his back problems during 1970, Young had been sitting around the ranch at La Honda, when the movie *Diary Of A Mad Housewife* came on his television screen. The story of a bored and repressed housewife who is married to a lawyer and who embarks on an affair before walking out on her husband, the lead role was played by the 24-year-old actress Carrie Snodgrass. With his marriage to Susan Acevado already over, Young describes what happened next in "A Man Needs A Maid".

A NEW LOVE IN YOUNG'S LIFE, ACTRESS CARRIE SNODGRASS.

"I fell in love with the actress, she was playing a part that I could understand." He obtained a phone number, rang her and left a message. Although she had never heard of Young or his music, Snodgrass was sufficiently intrigued to return the call and they arranged to meet. The rendezvous was cancelled when Young went into the Cedars of Lebanon hospital in LA for treatment on his back. Undeterred, Snodgrass visited his bedside and within weeks had moved in to the ranch at La Honda. By the time of *Harvest*'s release she was already pregnant with their son Zeke, who was born in September 1972.

Young recorded the song not in Nashville but on his visit to London in February 1971 when he hired the London Symphony Orchestra under conductor David Meecham to work with him at Barking Town Hall, one of the more unlikely locations for the making of rock history. Jack Nitzsche flew in to assist with the arrangement.

On the release of *Harvest*, "A Man Needs A Maid" was by far the album's most controversial track. The title sounded like something a male character in a Jane Austen novel might utter, rather than something that had any place in the politically correct, modern world. Clearly, Young's apparent desire for a housekeeper, "to keep my house clean, fix my meals and go away" was never going to make the song popular with the newly-emerging women's lib movement and many, in the feminist terminology of the time, dismissed him as a "male chauvinist pig".

In mitigation, the song was partly written while he was in hospital and unable to fend himself, so that, at the time, he did quite literally need a maid. "I found myself not being able to move around too much, in bed a lot, and my mind started wandering," he explained. "And when I got home I kept hearing this song over and over in my head."

But there are other nuances to the lyrics and a touching vulnerability to lines such as, "I don't know who to trust any more." Is the maid some kind of substitute for emotional involvement and how does Snodgrass fit into the equation? As often with Neil Young, the truth is more complicated than it at first appears.

Young was stung by the criticisms but took comfort from Dylan telling him he was a fan of the song. "I listened closer to Bob," he said, before suggesting people should not interpret the song too literally. "Robin Hood loved a maid long before women's liberation," he added.

HEART OF GOLD

"This song put me in the middle of the road," Young remarked of "Heart Of Gold", when he included it on the *Decade* anthology. A No. 1 single in America and top ten in Britain, the song has divided fans ever since, many of whom do not like Young in such overtly commercial mode. The writer Sylvie Simmons clams she "winces" every time she hears it.

The lyric may be trite and the rhyming scheme unimaginative. But at the very least, "Heart Of Gold" is a classic commercial pop song, as all those present in the studio were quick to recognize. The first track recorded during the Nashville sessions in February 1971, producer Elliott Mazer says it "wasn't part of the plan" to make a hit record. Yet he recalls that when Kenny Buttrey first heard Young play the song, he simply raised one finger in the air as if to say, "that's a number one record."

After the basic track had been recorded, James Taylor and Linda Ronstadt, who had been Young's fellow guests on the Johnny Cash show the day before and were still in town, added the harmony vocals.

The melody was evidently inspired by "Love Is Blue", a tune written by the French arranger Paul Mauriat, which was also recorded by the guitarist Jeff Beck.

"I'D HAPPENED TO BE IN THE RIGHT PLACE AT THE RIGHT TIME TO DO A REALLY MELLOW RECORD THAT WAS REALLY OPEN BECAUSE THAT WAS WHERE MY LIFE WAS AT THE TIME."

NEIL YOUNG

"I'd happened to be in the right place at the right time to do a really mellow record that was really open because that's where my life was at the time," Young later remarked. He soon came to regard the song and the commercial success it brought as an albatross. "I thought the record was good. But I knew something else was dying," he said.

ARE YOU READY FOR THE COUNTRY

Like "Cripple Creek Ferry" on *After The Gold Rush*, "Are You Ready For The Country" hints at a stronger story that the song itself never tells, particularly in the line, "I ran into the hangman, he said it's time to die."

"Are You Ready For The Country" is one of three tracks on Harvest that were worked on not in Nashville but in the studio that Young established in a barn at his La Honda ranch, where David Crosby and Graham Nash added backing vocals and Jack Nitzsche, the one non-Nashville-based member of the Stray Gators, added a rollicking piano part. They also ran a lead out into the valley adjacent to the ranch, and used it as a huge, natural echo chamber. According to Ben Keith, the sound could be heard "for miles".

OLD MAN

Young's father, Scott, a well-known Canadian sports writer and broadcaster who wrote a book called *Neil And Me*, initially believed "Old Man" had been written about him. In fact, the inspiration was Louis Avila, the foreman who worked on Young's La Honda ranch. "When I bought the place there was this old man who was working there for the people I bought it from. He was about 70 years old. He was a cattleman and that's like something that's never going to happen again," Young explained when introducing the song on stage. "So I wrote a song about it."

The lyric is tender and empathetic and the pedal steel guitar is complemented by a lovely rustic banjo, which may have been played by Young himself. Despite the lyric, "24 and there's so much more," Young was actually 26 when he wrote the song. Recorded in the same Nashville session as "Heart Of Gold", Taylor and Ronstadt again add backing vocals, but "Old Man" was to prove less successful as a single, only reaching No. 31 in the *Billboard* chart.

"SWEET BABY" JAMES TAYLOR'S BACKING VOCALS GRACED THE *HARVEST* ALBUM.

THERE'S A WORLD

Like "A Man Needs A Maid", Young recorded "There's A World" with the LSO in Barking Town Hall in February 1971. With its ludicrously grandiose arrangement by Jack Nitzsche, the introduction sounds like bad film music for a cheap B-movie and the tinkling harps and trilling flutes of the second section are difficult to ignore. The lyric makes a bid for some sort of profundity but is actually nonsensical. In short, there's little to commend the song, written in Vancouver a year or two earlier – although stripped of the orchestral bombast, the acoustic version he played on tour in 1970–71 sounded more acceptable.

ALABAMA

Picking up on the theme of "Southern Man" from *After The Gold Rush*, "Alabama" is a less angry swipe at the intolerance of the old South, which finds Young offering the hand of friendship "to help you along."

Not everybody appreciated the offer, and Lynyrd Skynyrd (who actually came from neighbouring Florida), responded by recording "Sweet Home Alabama", which amusingly put down Young for interfering where he was not wanted. Far from taking offence, he loved their riposte and later sent the band demos of several unrecorded songs for possible inclusion on a Lynyrd Skynyrd album.

When the band's singer Ronnie Van Zant, guitarist Steve Gaines and members of their road crew were killed in a plane crash on October 20, 1977, Young was deeply shocked. At a concert three weeks later, he paid tribute to their memory by singing "Sweet Home Alabama" as a medley with his own composition.

The version of "Alabama" on *Harvest* was recorded at Young's Broken Arrow ranch with the Stray Gators augmented with additional vocals by Stills and Crosby. It's also one of the two tracks on the album on which Young plays lead electric guitar, something that he had found physically impossible due to his back problems during earlier sessions for the album.

THE NEEDLE AND THE DAMAGE DONE

A stark contrast to anything else on *Harvest*, the stripped-down acoustic version of the junkie lament "The Needle And The Damage Done" was recorded live at a gig at the Royce Hall, UCLA.

Its inspiration had been the descent into heroin addiction of Danny Whitten, an issue that Young handles with great compassion. Whitten was still alive and so was capable of salvation, which is presumably why the song lacks the darker edge of some of Young's other drug songs which would later appear on *Tonight's The Night*.

The strongly autobiographical song's opening line, "I caught you knocking at my cellar door," plays on the double meaning of a junkie visiting his dealer and the Cellar Door club in Washington, where Young played with Whitten and Crazy Horse. The opening line of the second verse, "I hit the city and I lost my band" refers to Young sacking Crazy Horse due to Whitten's state during the early, aborted sessions for *After The Gold Rush*.

Some have complained that the song's final line, which compares a junkie to a "setting sun", romanticizes addiction by the use of an apparently appealing simile. This is unfair. When Young introduced the song at a concert in LA a year before its release, he told the audience with considerable sincerity, "This is a serious song I'd like to do about some people you know, some people I know and some people that neither one of us knows. It's about heroin addiction. Somewhere in the universe there's probably a place where all the great art is that didn't get out. A museum of incredible lost art that didn't get out because of heroin."

His anger at Whitten's decline was accentuated by its stupid, tragic waste, for Young not only valued him as a friend but rated him as a songwriter. The song has continued to feature in Young's repertoire and appeared on 1993's *Unplugged* album.

THE ROMANTIC TROUBADOUR – YOUNG FREQUENTLY PERFORMED ON HIS OWN IN CONCERT.

WORDS (BETWEEN THE LINES OF AGE)

There were times in his early career when Young appeared unduly in thrall to the influence of Bob Dylan. "The Last Trip To Tulsa" on his first solo album was one of them. "Words" was another. Lines such as "Someone and someone were down by the pond, looking for something to plant in the lawn" can only leave you wondering what on earth he's on about. "Living in castles a bit at a time, the king started laughing and talking in rhyme" sounds even more like a parody of Dylan at his most surreal, but without either the wit or invention. The lyrics drove Young's friend Jack Nitzsche to denounce them as "dumb and pretentious".

Unfortunately, at six-and-a-half minutes, "Words" is by far the longest song on the album, although it's less indulgent than the unforgivable 16-minute version on the soundtrack album, *Journey Through The Past*. Recorded with the Stray Gators in the barn at Young's ranch rather than in Nashville, the additional vocals of Stills and Nash, Young's most sinewy guitar playing on the record and an appealingly ramshackle rhythm save the track from total tedium, but it's a disappointing end to an otherwise great album.

TIME FADES AWAY

Recorded	Live in concert: January 1971 and January to April 1973: Cleveland, Ohio; Los Angeles, California; Oklahoma City, Oklahoma; Phoenix, Arizona; Sacramento, California; San Diego, California, Seattle, Washington.
Produced by	Neil Young, Elliot Mazer.
Musicians	Neil Young (vocals, lead guitar, piano, harmonica) Ben Keith (pedal steel guitar, backing vocals), Jack Nitzsche (piano), Johnny Barbata (drums), Tim Drummond (bass), Joe Yankee (bass), David Crosby (rhythm guitar, backing vocals), Graham Nash (rhythm guitar, backing vocals).

TIME FADES AWAY
JOURNEY THROUGH THE PAST
YONDER STANDS THE SINNER
L.A.
LOVE IN MIND
DON'T BE DENIED
THE BRIDGE
LAST DANCE

After *Harvest*, Young was a bona fide superstar who might easily have settled back in to safe musical conformity as a lovelorn, sensitive singer-songwriter and watched the royalties mount. However, while the world waited expectantly for a follow-up to the chart-topping "Heart Of Gold", Young had other ideas. The middle of the road was a boring place to travel and so, as he later put it, he "headed for the ditch".

"ONCE IN A WHILE I LIKE TO DO SOMETHING THAT HAS A CHANCE OF FAILING."
NEIL YOUNG

With an apparently capricious disregard for his career, his next move was to release the double album film soundtrack, *Journey Through The Past*. It was a critical and commercial disaster – and deservedly so. The album contained just one new song, "Soldier", versions of old Buffalo Springfield and CSNY songs, scrappy live versions of "Alabama" and "Words", plus inexplicable selections from Handel's Messiah and even a Beach Boys' instrumental. The album failed to dent the American top 40, a woeful fall from grace for an artist who had only six months earlier topped both singles and album charts. The film itself did not appear until long after the soundtrack album and was an unscripted mess with "no plot, no point and no stars," as Young himself confessed. "Once in a while I like to do something that has a chance of failing." In that at least, he spectacularly succeeded.

Bafflingly, the song from which the movie took its name and which Young had first played live during 1971 was not even included on the soundtrack. Instead, it appeared almost a year later in September 1973 on *Time Fades Away*, a live album consisting of new songs recorded on a disastrously unhappy stadium tour during which he stubbornly refused to play "Heart Of Gold," the one song his new mass audience most wanted to hear. Perversely, Young told Cameron Crowe in 1975 that he could easily have delivered "the perfect follow-up" to Harvest but declined to do so because his fans "would have thought that they understood what I was all about and that would have been it for me."

Instead he insisted, "You've got to keep changing. Shirts, old ladies, whatever. I'd rather keep changing and lose a lot of people along the way." He went on to claim he didn't care whether his audience was "a hundred or a hundred million", an attitude that helped contribute to the legend Young was fast building as one of the most independent-minded artists of his time – but which must have struck fear into his record company.

With hindsight, *Time Fades Away* can be seen as a powerful and courageous record. But it was not what fans of *Harvest* wanted or expected and Young has since disowned the recording, calling it the worst album of his career and refusing to allow its re-release on CD. "It's not something I want to listen to a lot. It makes you feel uneasy," he says.

TIME FADES AWAY

From the outset the omens for the tour on which the *Time Fades Away* album was recorded were ominous. Danny Whitten was back in the fold again, having promised that he had cleaned up his act. But after a few days of rehearsals, it was clear that he was more strung-out on heroin than ever and Young sacked him again. A day later, on November 18, 1972, Young received a call from the coroner to say that Whitten had been found dead in a bathroom from an overdose.

Although Young's ultimate elegy to Whitten would come on the spooky *Tonight's The Night* album, the ghostly presence of the late guitarist hung over the *Time Fades Away* tour which opened in January 1973. It rapidly became the tour from hell and the album's morbid title track, a bleak and nightmarish tale that opens with the line "fourteen junkies too weak to work" with pounding piano by Nitzsche characterizes the album's air of desperation.

Yet the spirit of doom derives as much from the style of the performances as the subject matter of the songs because Young had been singing much of the material on *Time Fades Away* for the previous two years without sounding like a man at the end of his tether.

JOURNEY THROUGH THE PAST

Omitted from the film soundtrack of the same name, "Journey Through The Past" was already established as a live favourite. Openly nostalgic for the Canada of Young's youth, a superb version played solo at the piano had long been available to collectors on a widely-circulated bootleg of his BBC2 "In Concert" performance recorded in February 1971, when he had introduced it as "another song I wrote about my home because I think about that a lot when I'm on the road." In truth, however, the rough version presented here fares poorly when compared to the powerfully restrained reading of earlier concerts.

The gentlest song on the album, "Journey Through The Past" contains a reference to fellow Canadian Joni Mitchell's composition, "The Fiddle and The Drum", which appeared on her 1969 album *Clouds*.

YOUNG HAS DISTANCED HIMSELF FROM *TIME FADES AWAY*, REFUSING TO SANCTION ITS DIGITAL REISSUE.

YONDER STANDS THE SINNER

There are a number of strong hints of atheism in Young's early work and he can be seen engaging a Jesus freak in animated debate in the *Journey Through The Past* film. In "Southern Man" he had angrily noted how "the good book" was used to justify prejudice and bigotry. There is considerable evidence that his views subsequently altered, particularly after the birth of his two disabled children, which he suggested in 1986 had made him feel that "God was trying to show me something." Yet, whatever the nature of his own faith, he has never had any time for organized religion. In the bluesy "Yonder Stands The Sinner", which he dubbed "bible rock", he suggests that the true sinners are not the ordinary, fallible human beings who are berated from the pulpit for their everyday failings but the moralizing hypocrites who are doing the preaching.

Young sounds totally hoarse, although there's an undeniable intensity about the performance and the coarseness of the recording accurately reflects the grim mood of the tour. Members of the Stray Gators were in almost open mutiny, fighting among themselves and demanding more money. Young was falling out badly with his old friend Jack Nitzsche. And then his voice started to give out. He sent for reinforcements in the form of Crosby and Nash, but they did little to help the demoralized mood of the tour. Crosby's mother was at the time dying of cancer and Nash was in shock after his girlfriend, Amy Gossage, had just been murdered by her brother. Could it get any worse? The answer was yes. Much. With *Time Fades Away*, Young was still only on part one of the series of albums that came to be known as "the doom trilogy".

L.A.

"Out on the West Coast people were beside palm trees, living by the ocean, worrying about earthquakes," Young remarked when introducing "L.A." on the BBC2 "In Concert" show, recorded in London in February 1971. He had long had a fascination with predictions of a Californian earthquake that would destroy Los Angeles and had been much taken with the narrative possibilities of such a disaster, which had been explored in Dean Stockwell's

WITH YOUNG'S 1973 TOUR FALLING APART AT THE SEAMS, HE SENT FOR THE BIG GUNS – DAVID CROSBY AND GRAHAM NASH.

screenplay of the unmade *After The Gold Rush* film.

"L.A." was written even earlier, in 1968, around the same time he wrote another ecological song, "Here We Are In The Years", which appeared on his solo debut. The song juxtaposes the superficial concerns of the inhabitants of the "uptight city in the smog" with their impending doom and appears to derive a perverse pleasure from the venomous invitation, "Don't you wish that you could be here, too?".

LOVE IN MIND

"I used to call this girl call from the road who I was in love with but I'd never really met. I used to talk to her on the phone all the time late at night because of the time difference and I'd wake up the next morning feeling so good," Young explained in introducing "Love In Mind" in concert. An unaccompanied piano ballad, the song sounds gentle enough, although its "what am I doing here?" refrain is perfectly in keeping with the album's generally frayed spirit.

Another song familiar from Young's BBC2 concert in London two-and-a-half years before it appeared on an official album, "Love In Mind" was written in Detroit, possibly as early as 1968. The song also has another dig at religious dogma and the church's attitude to sex.

THE WIDE OPEN PRAIRIE: "I THINK ABOUT MY HOME A LOT WHEN I'M ON THE ROAD," YOUNG TELLS US.

DON'T BE DENIED

Young's father, Scott, had divorced his wife Rassy when Neil was in his early teens, resulting in a move from Toronto to Winnipeg and a change of school. The teenager was deeply unhappy at Earl Grey Junior High School where he enrolled in 1960 and where he was mercilessly bullied. These events are chronicled in the unusually direct "Don't Be Denied".

Written at his ranch home in late His grief and self-reproach led him back to such familiar themes as the nature of fame and his ambivalent attitude to being a twentysomething millionaire superstar, making the song, in effect became a mini-autobiography of his life to date. The song remains a landmark in Young's canon and he was still performing "Don't Be Denied" into the 1990s with Crazy Horse.

THE BRIDGE

In the 1960s it was suggested that the Welsh poet Dylan Thomas would have been writing rock'n'roll lyrics if he had still been alive. His American equivalent was perhaps Hart Crane, an alcoholic poet who was born in Ohio in 1899 and committed suicide in 1932 by jumping from a steamer in the Caribbean, after spending some time in Mexico.

In his lifetime, he published two volumes of verse, *White Buildings* in 1926 and more significantly four years later *The Bridge*, a powerful exploration of the myth of America which included such characters as Christopher Columbus, Rip Van Winkle and Pocahontas and which has become a key text in twentieth-century American literature.

Young was reading *The Bridge* on his visit to London in early 1971 and immediately wrote a song with the same title. He performed the new work at the Festival Hall and introduced it with the words, "It started out like I was feeling I was Hart Crane, so I started writing this song about *The Bridge*. I wrote that here in the bustling city of London three days ago."

In Crane's poem, New York's Brooklyn Bridge becomes a symbol of the American experience and the Mississippi River is transformed into a natural force fusing history and the eternity of time. Young adapts the image in a more personalized way in the line, "And love came running down like a river on your skin and you let me in."

LAST DANCE

"This was the anti-Harvest tour," remembers Elliott Mazer, who was charged with recording every gig of the 1973 tour for the album that became *Time Fades Away*. "The more the audience would yell for 'Heart of Gold', 'Cinnamon Girl' and 'Old Man', the more he'd get mad and blast them with 15 minutes of 'Last Dance'."

The version of "Last Dance" preserved for posterity on *Time Fades Away* is dominated by Young's guitar playing, although his style was not always appreciated by his fractious musicians. "Everyone in the band was bored to death with those terrible guitar solos," Jack Nitzsche claimed. "He would turn and face the band with this stupid grimace while he was playing and I would nearly roll on the stage laughing."

Despite Nitzsche's harsh words, the two soon resumed their friendship. Young even appeared later to accept some of Nitzsche's criticisms as justified. "It was his opinion that I wasn't living up to my potential," Young told Nick Kent in 1995. "He was one of the guys who could see how fucked up I was compared to what I could really do."

With Crosby and Nash in tow, the song's commentary on the rat race and Young's proposed solution ("you can live your own life… laid back and laughing") is arguably as naive as anything the era of hippie idealism ever produced… or, if you're feeling as charitable as Young's biographer Johnny Rogan: "a cleverly executed ironic commentary on the fallacies of the hippie dream."

ON THE BEACH

Recorded	November 1973 to April 1974, Woodside and Hollywood, California.
Produced by	Neil Young, David Briggs, Mark Harman, Al Schmitt.
Musicians	Neil Young (vocals, guitar, electric piano, banjo, harmonica), Ben Keith (slide guitar, steel guitar, dobro, electric piano, organ, bass, hand drums), Tim Drummond (bass), Ralph Molina (drums) Additional Personnel: Billy Talbot (bass), Levon Helm (drums), Joe Yankee (harp, electric tambourine), David Crosby (guitar), Rick Danko (bass), George Whitsell (guitar), Graham Nash (electric piano), Rusty Kershaw (slide guitar, fiddle).

WALK ON
SEE THE SKY ABOUT TO RAIN
REVOLUTION BLUES
FOR THE TURNSTILES
VAMPIRE BLUES
ON THE BEACH
MOTION PICTURES (FOR CARRIE)
AMBULANCE BLUES

FAMILY MAN – NEIL YOUNG WITH SON ZEKE BACKSTAGE AT A CSNY CONCERT.

Young's follow-up album to *Time Fades Away* was scheduled to have been *Tonight's The Night*. Originally slated for release in January 1974, he had already toured many of the songs but it was another 18 months before the record eventually appeared. When it was withdrawn from the release schedules, it was rumoured that Reprise, appalled at Young's continuing failure to produce a commercial, radio-friendly follow-up to *Harvest*, had refused to put the album out.

Young later claimed that it was because the album simply wasn't finished. "It wasn't in the right space. It wasn't in the right order. The concept wasn't right," he said. The project was put on hold in favour of an entirely new collection of songs.

The album that jumped *Tonight's The Night* in the queue was *On The Beach*. Released in July 1974, the album came at the end of a difficult period for Young. His always delicate sense of equilibrium had been thrown horribly off-kilter by the death of his friend Danny Whitten from a heroin overdose and the similar death of one of his roadies, Bruce Berry. An attempt to record another CSNY album, *Human Highway*, had collapsed amid egos and acrimony. The *Tonight's The Night* tour of Britain at the end of 1973 had been a shambolic disaster, with audience reaction ranging from incomprehension to anger.

From this unpromising twilight zone emerged *On The Beach*, a striking series of glimpses into the deepest recesses of his soul and, to this critic at least, one of the finest albums of his career. When first released, however, *On The Beach* was widely misunderstood by reviewers who saw it as a work of unremitting bleakness and self-pity. Even *Rolling Stone*, which rated the album highly, still called it "one of the most despairing works of the decade."

Certainly, themes of paranoia, the corrosive nature of celebrity and the death of the hippie dream were not the stuff of easy-listening. It is also true that three of the eight songs have the word "blues" in their titles, with all the connotations that suggests. Yet the album possesses a far wider vision than many recognized at the time and Johnny Rogan is surely right to herald it as a move on Young's part away from the darkness of *Time Fades Away* and the still-to-be-released T*onight's The Night* "towards a belief that something positive might ultimately emerge from the chaos."

Whatever its emotional and psychological provenance, *On The Beach* restored Young to the American top 20, although the record fared less well in Britain, where the catastrophic *Tonight's The Night* tour had demolished his reputation. Released during the middle of a CSNY reunion tour, Young displayed his under-rated sense of humour when he mischievously described the album as "like a wart or something on the perfect beast."

Interestingly enough, for a long time – until 2003 – Young refused to allow *On The Beach* to be issued on CD.

WALK ON

It was odd that so many critics should dismiss *On The Beach* as a work of unremitting gloom and despair when the album opened with the positively jaunty "Walk On". Recorded at Young's Broken Arrow ranch with the old Crazy Horse rhythm section of Talbot and Molina plus the Stray Gators' Ben Keith on slide guitar, Young later claimed the song was a "defensive reaction to criticisms of *Tonight's The Night*". His memory was playing tricks, for the song actually pre-dated the *Tonight's The Night* tour, having first been performed live in August 1973. It was then recorded at the sessions intended to complete the *Tonight's The Night* album before being pressed into service for *On The Beach*.

Lines such as "I hear some people been talkin' me down" represent a spirited riposte to critics who savaged *Time Fades Away*, and the general tone is some way from the hopelessness that the album is often said to convey.

SEE THE SKY ABOUT TO RAIN

One of the recurring themes of Young's long career is the reworking of old songs. "See The Sky About To Rain" had been around as a live favourite for at least three years before its appearance on *On The Beach* and had been recorded by the Byrds on their 1973 reunion album, presumably at David Crosby's instigation.

Having failed to find room on *Harvest* or *Time Fades Away*, Young finally decided the song fitted his more meditative mood and re-recorded it with himself on Wurlitzer piano, Tim Drummond from the Stray Gators on bass, The Band's Levon Helm on drums and Ben Keith adding some lovely pedal steel. The snatch of harmonica at the very end is credited to Joe Yankee, a pseudonym for none other than Young himself, who had used the name before when playing on other people's records.

THE NOTORIOUS CULT LEADER CHARLES MANSON HAD BEEN A FRIEND OF BOTH NEIL YOUNG AND DENNIS WILSON.

REVOLUTION BLUES

One of the reasons that Young for so long excised *On The Beach* from his available catalogue may have been that he does not wish to be reminded of his friendship with the notorious mass murderer Charles Manson, who inspired "Revolution Blues."

Young had met Manson at the home of Beach Boy Dennis Wilson in 1968 and was fascinated by the crazed cult leader and the coterie of adoring hippie chicks around him known as "The Family". "He was potentially a poet," he told Nick Kent in his book *The Dark Stuff*. "The girls were around, too. They were always there. They'd be right on the couch with me, singing a song. And Charlie would talk to me about how he'd been in jail so much that there was no longer any difference being in or out of jail." Young even suggested to Reprise boss Mo Ostin that he might sign Manson as a singer-songwriter, claiming he was "unique... special... really, really good."

A year later, in the summer of 1969, Manson launched a horrific murder spree, despatching the Family to the Beverly Hills home of film director Roman Polanski, where they massacred his pregnant actress wife Sharon Tate and four others. Two days later they struck again at another wealthy Hollywood home. Manson's arrest and the subsequent trial was another nail in the coffin of the Californian hippie dream. The funeral was to come at the end of that year in the violence and death meted out by Hell's Angels thugs at the Altamont festival, where CSNY were one of the bands on a bill headed by the Rolling Stones.

Young's acquaintance with Manson was brief. He soon found him "too intense" and felt he had to "get out this guy's way before he explodes." Clearly, he had enjoyed a narrow escape, although when news of the murders broke, Young did not at first make the connection. "When it first came out there'd been this horrible murder and the guy's name was Charles Manson, I never put it all together with this other guy Charlie that I'd known," he admitted.

In "Revolution Blues" Young satirizes the traumatic events surrounding Manson's crimes quite brilliantly, although not everybody appreciated the black humour of the image of "blood fountains", let alone the final line, "I hear that Laurel Canyon is full of famous stars, but I hate them worse than lepers and I'll kill them in their cars."

When Young wanted to sing the song on CSNY's 1974 tour, his colleagues were reluctant. "They didn't know if they wanted to stand on the same stage as me when I was doing it," he told Nick Kent a decade and a half later. "I was going, 'It's just a fuckin' song. What's the big deal? It's about the culture. It's about what's really happening.'"

Despite his reservations, the *On The Beach* version features David Crosby on second guitar supporting Young's lead lines and a rhythm section provided by Levon Helm and Rick Danko from The Band.

FOR THE TURNSTILES

Young has always shown a healthy contempt for the "suits" who run the record industry and "For The Turnstiles" expresses his preoccupation with the battle between commerce and art with considerable eloquence.

Fittingly, the song eschews standard pop/rock instrumentation and features just banjo and dobro as he describes the experience of "singing songs for pimps with tailors who charge ten dollars at the door." He wonders how he can retain his integrity in the face of this prostitution of his art.

VAMPIRE BLUES

In 1973–74 there was a global oil crisis, prompted by a massive 70 per cent price hike imposed by OPEC (Organization of Petroleum Exporting Countries). In the volatile trading conditions this created, fortunes could be made and lost and it was against this background that Young wrote "Vampire Blues" in which he assumes the persona of an oil magnate "sucking blood from the earth." There was an added irony in the fact that the vinyl from which his records were manufactured was an oil by-product.

Musically, the song is an undistinguished blues, featuring members of both Crazy Horse and the Stray Gators, with the addition of George Whitsell from The Rockets on guitar.

ON THE BEACH

Side two of *On The Beach* features just three songs – "On The Beach", "Motion Pictures" and "Ambulance Blues" – constituting a sustained and coherent commentary on fame and the price it exacts. The subject matter could have sounded whining and self-pitying but Young carries it off brilliantly through a combination of emotional honesty and an intuitive touch that makes the sequence one of the crowning achievements of his career. Indeed, for many years, *On The Beach* ranked with Tim Buckley's *Starsailor* as among the most significant albums not to have been made available in any of the new digital formats.

The sequence opens with the album's title track, in which the world is "turning" and leaving a stoned-sounding Young out of step. At the song's core is the paradox of the artist who "needs a crowd of people" but "can't face them day to day." Essentially a 12-bar blues, the song is slowed down to an enervated shuffle with Graham Nash on piano and Young playing compelling lead guitar.

MOTION PICTURES (FOR CARRIE)

The stoned mood that dominates side two is maintained on "Motion Pictures" and Young subsequently explained how the album had been made on a diet of "honey slides", marijuana lightly cooked in melted honey. Indeed, one of his favourite party pieces at the time was to give audiences a detailed recipe between songs during live shows.

The song is dedicated to Carrie Snodgrass, his actress partner who had given up her movie career to bring up their son Zeke. Shortly after the release of *On The Beach* she moved out of Young's Broken Arrow ranch and the first cracks in their relationship are already apparent from the opening line, which finds him away from home, watching TV in a motel room and "living in between".

Yet the song is not only about his relationship with Snodgrass but is also an inner monologue on his own career. He still has his "dreams" but they have little to do with the superficiality of rock stardom, he insists. The slide guitar is played by Rusty Kershaw, who also contributes some decidedly eccentric liner notes to the original album.

AMBULANCE BLUES

The album's closing song and tour de force is a dazzling trip around Young's history and the state of the world, set against a simple finger-picking guitar arrangement. It opens in a straightforwardly nostalgic vein with Young reminiscing about "the old folkie days" in the Riverboat coffee house in Toronto and his former rented home at 88 Isabella Street. But the theme of impermanence that also dominates the album's title track rears its head again and says "proud Isabella" has been torn down.

From there, the imagery gets more complex via the Navajo trial, Mother Goose and a reference to the 1974 kidnapping by left-wing radicals of the newspaper heiress Patty Hearst, whose grandfather William Randolph Hearst had been the inspiration for Orson Welles' film *Citizen Kane*. There are further observations on the nature of fame and Young's see-saw career trajectory and another reply to his critics, "you're no better than me for what you've shown."

AMERICA'S MOST WANTED: WILLIAM AND EMILY HARRIS AND PATTY HEARST – THE SYMBIONESE LIBERATION ARMY.

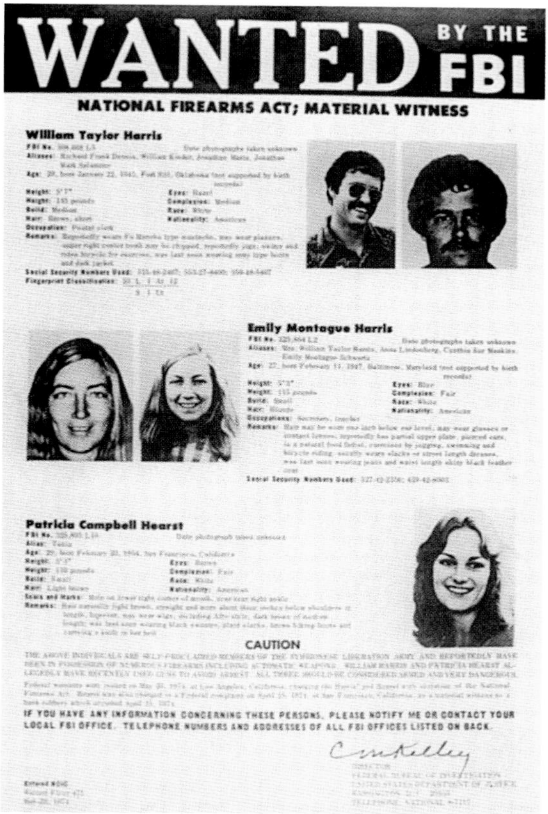

The song's most famous line, "You're all just pissing in the wind", is a quote from Young's manager Elliott Roberts, and a remark he allegedly made about CSNY and their monstrously clashing egos. Finally, there's a parting shot at disgraced president Richard Nixon ("I never knew a man could tell so many lies") at a time when the Watergate scandal and his subsequent impeachment were dominating the news.

The accompaniment is compelling but simple, allowing the focus to rest on the lyric, while Kershaw's extraordinary fiddle enhances the mood. The closest parallel in terms of the song's panoramic scope is, perhaps, Dylan's "Desolation Row" and a number of critics, including Ian MacDonald in *NME*, Stephen Holden in *Rolling Stone* and Johnny Rogan in his biography *Zero To Sixty*, have all suggested that "Ambulance Blues" may be the pinnacle of Young's entire recording career.

TONIGHT'S THE NIGHT

Recorded	December 1972 to December 1973, Woodside and Hollywood, California; "Come on Baby Let's Go Down" recorded live at Fillmore East, New York City, March 1970.
Produced by	Neil Young, David Briggs, Tim Mulligan, Elliot Mazer.
Musicians	Neil Young (vocals, piano, guitar, harmonica, vibes) Ben Keith (pedal steel guitar, vocals, slide guitar), Nils Lofgren (guitar, piano, vocal), Danny Whitten (guitar, vocals), Jack Nitzsche (electric piano, piano), Billy Talbot (bass), Tim Drummond (bass), Ralph Molina drums, vocals), Kenny Buttrey (drums), George Whitsell (vocal).

TONIGHT'S THE NIGHT
SPEAKIN' OUT
WORLD ON A STRING
BORROWED TUNE
COME ON BABY LET'S GO DOWN
MELLOW MY MIND
ROLL ANOTHER NUMBER (FOR THE ROAD)
ALBUQUERQUE
NEW MAMA
LOOKOUT JOE
TIRED EYES

TONIGHT'S THE NIGHT WAS A DIRECT EXPRESSION OF YOUNG'S GRIEF AT THE DEATHS OF DANNY WHITTEN AND BRUCE BERRY.

To pick up the story of *Tonight's The Night*, we must first turn back to August 1973, before the release of *On The Beach*. CSNY had assembled at Young's ranch to continue work on an album they planned to name *Human Highway*. The initial sessions held in Hawaii in June had gone well.

Yet two months later, the spirit of camaraderie had somehow evaporated and the La Honda sessions descended once again into bickering. Young looked at them, saw a bunch of small-minded, pampered superstars and decided that he'd had enough.

On his way to a CSNY session for which his enthusiasm had evaporated, he stopped off to call on his old producer David Briggs, who had just returned to northern California after two years in Canada. Young told Briggs he couldn't face the CSNY album and announced he was going to miss the session. "Let's go make some rock'n'roll," he said.

"So we packed our bags," Briggs later recalled to Neil's father, Scott Young, "and came down to LA and wound up with *Tonight's The Night*."

Calling on the services of his old Crazy Horse colleagues Ralph Molina and Billy Talbot, Young also rounded up old friends Ben Keith and Nils Lofgren and dubbed the band The Santa Monica Flyers. Working at LA's Studio Instrument Rentals, the sessions followed a regular daily pattern. Young and the group would spend the afternoon drinking and smoking weed and getting "weird and wasted". Then when he felt they were in the twilight zone he was looking for, the tapes would start running.

By then, Bruce Berry, an old friend and a CSNY guitar roadie, had joined Danny Whitten on the roll call of heroin victims and Young later spoke of the sessions as "a wake" for Berry and Whitten. They worked fast and spontaneously. In one night they recorded five songs – "Tonight's The Night", "World On A String", "Mellow My Mind", "Speakin' Out" and "Tired Eyes". Eventually, they had nine tracks, raw and livid, many of them obsessed with heroin and death. As a record, *Tonight's The Night* was harrowing and uncompromising, a festering exorcism that could not have been further from the gently lapping tunes of *After The Gold Rush* or *Harvest*.

There are different stories about what happened next. Young's record label was appalled by what they heard and there were rumours that they had point blank refused to put the record out. Young refuted this version when the album was eventually released, insisting that the delay was because the record was unfinished. Yet some pressure clearly was brought to bear for he also told *Melody Maker*'s Allan Jones, "I was 'advised' that if I put out *Tonight's The Night* it would be suicidal for my career."

"IT'S THE BLACK SHEEP OF THE FAMILY… I JUST LIKE IT."
NEIL YOUNG (ON *TONIGHT'S THE NIGHT*)

Although the album remained unreleased, Young took the songs on the road for a series of bizarre concerts. Between the songs he rambled incoherently, obviously stoned or drunk, or both. The tour was regarded as a disaster and some speculated that Young was about to join Whitten and Berry. One news wire even carried a report of his demise, causing his father to ring and check on his son's health.

Yet instead of crashing, the tour appeared to exorcise some of his demons and he left *Tonight's The Night* behind and recorded and released *On The Beach*.

If Reprise, his record label, hoped that he had forgotten all about *Tonight's The Night*, they had another think coming. After recording another, more melodic album called *Homegrown*, and then cancelling its release at the last moment (it has remained in the vaults to this day), Young announced to Reprise that he wanted finally to go ahead and release *Tonight's The Night*. The decision was taken one night at his new home on Zuma beach, where he played both albums to friends, including The Band's Rick Danko and Levon Helm. Fuelled by alcohol and who knows what else, the assembled throng told Young that *Tonight's The Night* was more worthy of release.

Reprise attempted to dissuade him and, when that failed, then asked him to remix the record. Again Young refused. "I told them to shove it up their ass," he said later. "They could take it the way it was or they would never hear from me again."

With the addition of three further tracks, the album was eventually released 23 months after it was recorded. Critics and fans alike were shocked by its nakedness and audacious honesty. Today it stands as one of the great masterpieces in Young's canon and a record the artist himself has often cited as his favourite. "It's the black sheep of the family," he said in 1981. "I just like it."

TONIGHT'S THE NIGHT

Young dedicated the album to both Danny Whitten and Bruce Berry "who lived and died for rock'n'roll." But the title track, versions of which both open and close the record, is specifically about the hapless Berry.

The brother of Jan Berry of the surf duo Jan and Dean, Bruce Berry had been well-liked by Young, until his heroin habit diminished his ability to function. Young learned of Berry's death on his return from Hawaii in June 1973, where he had been recording with CSNY.

The song had begun life in the studio as little more than a spontaneous chorus around the repeated refrain, "Tonight's the night". The next day, Young turned up with the words about Berry and it was recorded straight away. Sounding fragile, vulnerable and close to panic, Young repeats the title line eight times before telling Berry's story, paying tribute to him as "a working man" and a musician who was "as real as the day is long".

At one point, Young even hatched a plan for a stage musical based around the life of a roadie modelled on Berry, titled *From Roadie To Riches*. A rough treatment was written although the project ultimately came to nothing. "For Broadway in 1974 it was a little ahead of its time," Young told Nick Kent in *Mojo* in 1996.

SPEAKIN' OUT

Young has always rejected the notion that *Tonight's The Night* is a totally downbeat record. "There's always a chance that nobody will dig it because it's too abrasive, but it's a very happy record if you're loose," he said. Despite its somewhat maudlin blues sound, lyrically "Speakin' Out" contains a healthy dose of optimism. It opens with Young taking in a movie, eating popcorn and "looking for good times." He then finds the possibility of redemption in fatherhood, celebrating the birth of his first son, Zeke, "you're holding my baby and I'm holding you." The guitar solo is played not by Young, but by Nils Lofgren.`

LONG-STANDING SIDEMAN NILS LOFGREN ENJOYED A SUCCESSFUL SOLO CAREER OF HIS OWN DURING THE 1970S.

WORLD ON A STRING

The jaunty "World On A String" returns to the familiar theme of the vicissitudes of fame and reflects Young's refusal to live up to the career expectations that the success of "Heart Of Gold" and *Harvest* had created. "I knew what I was doing wasn't what people wanted to hear. But I couldn't give them what they wanted," Young explained later. "I'm not going to grow if I'm just giving people what they think they want to hear from me. I'm gonna die."

BORROWED TUNE

As the title suggests – and as Young brazenly admits in the lyric – "Borrowed Tune" plagiarizes the Rolling Stones' "Lady Jane", although Jagger and Richards do not receive credits as co-writers.

"Borrowed Tune" was one of the three songs added to the original nine tracks recorded for Tonight's The Night in 1973. However, it was not a later song but an earlier one, having been recorded in 1972 immediately after the death of Whitten with the Stray Gators while rehearsing for the *Time Fades Away* tour. The vocal finds Young at his most frayed and torn – "too wasted", as he admits in the song, to write his own tune.

COME ON BABY LET'S GO DOWN

The addition of "Come On Baby Let's Go Down" to the album was a master stroke. Recorded live with Crazy Horse at the Fillmore East in 1970, the song features Whitten singing a song he had written about being a junkie, two years before the dope finally killed him. It may not be a Neil Young song, but its presence on *Tonight's The Night* is integral to the album's concept.

Whitten had died of an overdose on November 18, 1972, immediately after being fired by Young at the start of rehearsals for *Time Fades Away* with the Stray Gators. Worse still, he had died after shooting up dope he had scored with the 50 dollars Young had given him when he sacked him. Young recalled the circumstances to Cameron Crowe in *Rolling Stone* after *Tonight's The Night* was released: "We were rehearsing with him and he just couldn't cut it. He couldn't remember anything. He was too far gone. I had to tell him to go back to LA. 'It's not happening, man. You're not together enough.' He just said, 'I've got nowhere else to go, man. How am I gonna tell my friends?' And he split. That night the coroner called me from LA and told me he's OD'd. That blew my mind. Fucking blew my mind. I loved Danny. I felt responsible."

MELLOW MY MIND

"I know that the first time I heard *Tonight's The Night* it was the most out of tune thing I'd ever heard," Young once admitted. And nowhere is he more off-key than on "Mellow My Mind". It's obvious he's completely out of it and his voice cracks and croaks, strains and breaks. Technically, it's embarrassing – and yet it's utterly compelling.

Originally intended for CSNY, Young described the song as being about wanting to escape from the rock'n'roll lifestyle of being on the road. It was later covered by Mick Hucknall and Simply Red.

ROLL ANOTHER NUMBER (FOR THE ROAD)

Young had been ambivalent about CSNY's appearance at the Woodstock festival in 1969, when they had been helicoptered in for their second ever appearance as a quartet. "I wasn't really into it. It was so big and everything. I don't know what we were doing," he said afterwards. On "Roll Another Number (For The Road)" he takes another stoned and sardonic sideswipe at the spirit of Woodstock, opining "I'm a million miles away from that helicopter day and I don't think I'll be going back that way." For Young, the deaths of Whitten and Berry meant that the hippie dream was well and truly over.

ALBUQUERQUE

"What we were doing was playing those guys on their way. We all got high," Young said in describing the *Tonight's The Night* sessions. "We'd get really high, drink a lot of tequila, get right out on the edge, where we knew we were so screwed up that we could easily just fall on our faces and not be able to handle it as musicians. But we were open at that time." On "Albuquerque", which finds Young "rolling another number", you can hear exactly the mood he describes.

NEW MAMA

"New Mama" had been written with CSNY in mind, but when *Human Highway*, the planned follow-up to Deja Vu, was abandoned, Young got Crazy Horse to add some very creditable CSN style harmonies. It's a lovely song, a moment of respite in the drug-induced desperation, written for Carrie Snodgrass on the birth of their son, Zeke, in September 1972. Whitten overdosed just ten weeks later, and the contrast of birth and death – two sides of the same human coin – clearly struck Young forcibly, hence the inclusion of the song on *Tonight's The Night*.

By the time the album was released, Snodgrass and Zeke had moved out of the ranch at La Honda. "Carrie seeks the simple things that I sing about and have trouble reaching," Young wrote to his father. He's seldom sung about them with as much frazzled beauty as he sums up on "New Mama." Stephen Stills also recorded the song on his 1975 album *Stills*.

LOOKOUT JOE

Addressed to a "G.I. Joe" returning from the Vietnam, "Look Out Joe" warns the battle-scarred solider that he may be stepping out of one war and into another one, a nightmarish vision of an America populated by heroin addicts, strung-out hip drag queens, street walkers and dealers.

Like "Borrowed Tune", the song was recorded in November 1972 with the Stray Gators, just after Whitten's death. "He'd been working on the song with us and after he died we stopped for a while," Young recalls. "When we started playing again that was the first thing we cut."

TIRED EYES

There is a view that holds *Tonight's The Night* is far more than just a wake for two friends who died from heroin overdoses. In this broader scheme, the album becomes an epitaph for an America that has lost its moral compass and for its dead in the jungles of Vietnam as well as in the back streets and barrios of urban America.

YOUNG WARNED TROOPS RETURNING FROM VIETNAM THAT A DIFFERENT WAR MAY AWAIT THEM BACK HOME.

"Lookout Joe" hints at this universality and "Tired Eyes" also widens the focus beyond Berry and Whitten by describing a brutal LA murder in a cocaine deal gone wrong. The war has come home with a vengeance – a theme that John Prine also took up in his brilliant Vietnam veteran song "Sam Stone".

Young's performance on "Tired Eyes" has a world-weary lethargy so that the song is oddly drained of tension and drama. Paradoxically, this only adds to its impact. "I think this is one of my strongest and longest lasting albums," Young said in 1977. "It covers my obsession with the ups and downs of the drug culture. Coincidentally, it was my least commercially successful record."

ZUMA/LONG MAY YOU RUN

ZUMA

Recorded	Redwood City and Point Dume, California.
Produced by	Neil Young, David Briggs, Tim Mulligan.
Musicians	Neil Young with Crazy Horse: Neil Young (vocals, guitar), Frank Sampedro (rhythm guitar), Billy Talbot (bass, vocals), Ralph Molina (drums, vocals) Additional personnel: Tim Drummond (bass), David Crosby (vocals), Stephen Stills (bass, vocals), Graham Nash (vocals), Russ Kunkel (congas).

DON'T CRY NO TEARS; DANGER BIRD; PARDON MY HEART; LOOKIN' FOR A LOVE; BARSTOOL BLUES; STUPID GIRL; DRIVE BACK; CORTEZ THE KILLER: THROUGH MY SAILS

LONG MAY YOU RUN (THE STILLS-YOUNG BAND)

Recorded	February to June 1976, Miami, Florida.
Produced by	Tom Dowd, Don Gehman, Stephen Stills, Neil Young.
Musicians	Neil Young (vocals, guitar, keyboards), Stephen Stills (vocals, guitar, piano), Joe Lala (percussion, vocals), Jerry Aiello (keyboards), George "Chocolate" Perry (bass, vocals), Joe Vitale (drums, flute, vocals).

LONG MAY YOU RUN; MIDNIGHT ON THE BAY; OCEAN GIRL; LET IT SHINE; FOUNTAINBLEAU

A NEW VERSION OF CRAZY HORSE EMERGED FOR THE RECORDING OF *ZUMA*.

After the release of *Tonight's The Night* in 1975, Young finally put behind him the depression and heavy drinking that had followed the deaths of Bruce Berry and Danny Whitten. His relationship with Carrie Snodgrass had not survived this dark period, but he did not seem unduly bothered and enthusiastically embraced bachelorhood, taking a house on Zuma Beach, Malibu, which had once been owned by F. Scott Fitzgerald, the writer of *The Great Gatsby*. The beach house was conveniently situated near to the new home of his producer David Briggs and Young also turned again for support to some of his oldest musical associates. Over the next year, he recorded new albums with both Stephen Stills and Crazy Horse.

Without Danny Whitten, the future of Crazy Horse had seemed uncertain. But when the surviving rhythm section of Talbot and Molina found a replacement guitarist in Frank Sampedro, they anxiously invited Young to meet their new colleague. They hit it off and by the end of their first jam session together, Young had enlisted the new Crazy Horse line-up to play on his next record. The album that was eventually to emerge as *Zuma* went through several incarnations before its release in November 1975. Fascinated by the impact of the arrival of Christopher Columbus and other Europeans on America's indigenous Indian tribes, Young had first announced an album called *Ride My Llama*. "It's about the Incas and the Aztecs," he enthused. "It's like being in another civilization. It's a lost sort of soul form that switches from history scene to history scene trying to find itself."

The album went through further title changes, including *My Old Neighbour* and *My Old Car*, before he settled on *Zuma*. In the event, the only songs that related to his initial concept were "Cortez The Killer" and the title, not only the name of the beach where Young was living but also a reference to the Aztec emperor Montezuma. When the album was released less than six months after *Tonight's The Night*, it was warmly received by the critics, many of whom were glad that it marked a break with the uncomfortable listening of the so-called "doom trilogy" that had begun with *Time Fades Away* and had continued through *On The Beach* and *Tonight's The Night*.

However, even before *Zuma* was released, Young had embarked on a fresh project which found him resuming relations with his old sparring partner, Stephen Stills. Forced to cancel a tour with Crazy Horse after doctors had ordered him to rest his voice, he turned up at a Stills gig in July 1975 and played guitar. They duo immediately began to plan an album together.

STEPHEN STILLS, YOUNG'S PERENNIAL COLLABORATOR.

The tour with Crazy Horse, which had been rescheduled for November, intervened. But almost as soon as it was over, Young and Stills went into the studio in January 1976, making rapid progress and recording a dozen songs. Of course, as ever when Young and Stills got together, nothing was that straightforward. First, they decided to get Crosby and Nash in to sing backing harmonies. Then, after two weeks of sessions, Young and Stills decided they didn't want their old colleagues on the record after all. Crosby and Nash's contributions were wiped from the tapes, causing one of the biggest fractures ever in the CSNY camp. Stills attempted to explain the decision by claiming that they had decided that if the four of them were going to make a record together, then it should be a full-scale CSNY album. A furious Nash – usually the mildest of the quartet and the peacemaker – declared he would never work with them again.

The Stills-Young Band's album *Long May You Run* appeared in September 1976. Containing just nine songs, five of them by Young, it was pleasant but hardly the glorious reunion that Buffalo Springfield fans might have been anticipating. By the time the album was released, the restless Young had already moved on, pulling out of a three-month tour with the Stills-Young Band after just 18 days. He simply turned his bus around on the way to a gig in Atlanta and stopped off to wire Stills from a telegram office on his way home to California. "Dear Stephen, funny how some things that start spontaneously end that way. Eat a peach, Neil," said the curt message.

He later dismissed the Stills-Young Band record as "an attempt to wrap up something that we had started a long time ago. It really wasn't as hot as the early stuff we did."

DON'T CRY NO TEARS

Young's first serious group, the Squires, was formed in a Winnipeg basement towards the end of 1962, just as the Beatles were emerging from Liverpool's Cavern Club to change the face of popular music. Young was 16 and although the group played mostly covers, he had also started writing his own songs. They included "I Wonder", influenced by the new sound of Merseybeat emanating from England. The Squires played the song on a couple of local radio stations in 1964 and it featured on the demo that was turned down by the Canadian division of Capitol Records. The following year, Young reworked the song as "Don't Pity Me Babe" for his solo Elektra audition in New York. The song then lay dormant for more than a decade until it reappeared as "Don't Cry No Tears" on *Zuma*. The composition retains an innocent, early-1960s feel and is a pleasing but slight opening to the album, although it serves as an instant illustration of how well the new guitarist Frank Sampedro had bedded in to the Crazy Horse line-up.

DANGER BIRD

Whenever Young's career reached a crossroads, he would usually call up his Crazy Horse colleagues. The group, he insisted, gave him "the possibilities of doing more with my guitar and voice than anybody else." The death of Danny Whitten had changed the group's chemistry, "but not the overall feeling of what we were about."

"Danger Bird" finds Crazy Horse at their brooding best and recalls the sound they had first perfected with Whitten. Written in the wake of Young's fractured relationship with Carrie Snodgrass, the line "Danger bird, he flies alone" recalls the imagery of *The Loner*.

PARDON MY HEART

"This is the first time I can remember coming out of a relationship definitely not wanting to get into another one," Young told *Rolling Stone*'s Cameron Crowe in 1975. But he did reflect on what had happened in a series of songs, and there can be little doubt that the poignant acoustic ballad "Pardon My Heart" was written with Snodgrass in mind.

"Everything worked out just as we had planned from the beginning," Snodgrass told a New York journalist in 1977. "We always said that when one of us wanted to end it, we would end it. We never had bad times and we still see each other." That the couple had a son, Zeke, of course, made continued contact inevitable. But she sounded puzzled as to what had gone wrong. "One day he came back and said he thought it was time for me to leave," she recalled. "I don't know why we broke up. We never fought."

"Pardon My Heart" had been premiered on the 1974 CSNY tour. On the recorded version, the backing vocals of Crazy Horse's Talbot and Molina may be less polished than those of Crosby, Stills and Nash, but they are every bit as effective.

LOOKIN' FOR A LOVE

A fantasy about meeting an idealized lover on a beach, "where the sun hits the water and the mountains meet the sand", the jaunty, country-ish sound of "Lookin' For A Love" would not have sounded out of place on *Harvest*. The beach sounds like *Zuma* itself, just a stone's throw from David Briggs's house where Young and Crazy Horse rehearsed for the album.

BARSTOOL BLUES

While recording *Zuma*, Crazy Horse's Frank Sampedro recalled a night spent touring every bar in Malibu with Young. "He was feeling real down and he was going to go home and feel lousy. So I said 'come on, Neil, let's go out and get drunk,'" he recalled in 1980 to *Trouser Press*.

The following day, Young announced that he couldn't remember having written them, but he had woken up with three new songs. One of them was "Bar Stool Blues". Young's depression that had led Sampedro to suggest a drinking spree is still evident, and there's even a touch of self-loathing in the lines "His life was filled with parasites and countless idle threats, he trusted in a woman and on her he made his bets."

STUPID GIRL

How on earth did the story get about that "Stupid Girl" had been written about Joni Mitchell? Nobody seems certain, and yet the notion has been common currency in rock circles for many years now. Neither Young's principal biographer Johnny Rogan nor Karen O'Brien in *Shadows and*

JONI MITCHELL – COULD "STUPID GIRL" *REALLY* HAVE BEEN ABOUT HER?

Light, her definitive study of Mitchell, are able to find any evidence to support the suggestion.

Young and Mitchell had first met at the 4D coffee house in Winnipeg in 1964 and had much in common, including not only their musical interests and Canadian prairie roots but the survival of childhood bouts of polio. "I felt very kindred to Neil," Mitchell says, and wrote "The Circle Game" as a direct reply to his song "Sugar Mountain", which he had composed on his twenty-first birthday and sung on his Elektra demo in 1965. Young also wrote Mitchell an affectionate song called "Sweet Joni" in the early 1970s, which has still never been released. The suggestion that he should then turn on her as the "stupid girl" who's "really got a lot to learn" appears to be little more than a malicious invention.

Which raises one very big question: if not Joni, then who *was* the song about? Since Young certainly isn't telling, we shall probably never know the answer.

DRIVE BACK

If "Pardon My Heart" and "Lookin' For A Love" illustrated Young the romantic, then "Stupid Girl" and "Drive Back" represent his more cynical side. The lyrics of "Drive Back" deal with a broken relationship, but with a sting that recalls the viciousness of some of Dylan's mid-1960s lyrics such as "Like A Rolling Stone" and "Positively 4th Street", in which old friends and lovers are cast aside with an almost malicious glee.

CORTEZ THE KILLER

The Spanish conquistador Hernan Cortez (sometimes spelt Cortes) invaded Mexico in 1519 with a band of just 600 men. He burnt his boats before marching to the Aztec capital Tenochtitlan, taking the ships' guns with him. The Aztec emperor Montezuma at first refused the Spaniards entry to the city, which was built on a lake and reached by a causeway. But Cortez would not be denied, attracted by the riches of gold within the city. When Montezuma reluctantly allowed him in, the Aztecs revolted, Montezuma was murdered and Cortez was forced to fight his way out of the city, losing a third of his men in the process. The Spaniards then besieged and bombarded Tenochtitlan and the Aztecs, already weakened by smallpox, which had been

brought by the Spaniards from Cuba, surrendered. Within two years of Cortez's arrival, an entire civilization had been virtually destroyed in what we would today call genocide.

Young's version of the story is a highly romanticized one, painting a picture of the Aztecs living in an earthly paradise where "war was never known" and "the people worked together". Of course, as is well known, the Aztecs practised human sacrifice to appease their gods – which was one of the reasons that several other local tribes readily joined Cortez against them. Young recognizes this fact in his lyric, but invests the practice with a false nobility, insisting the sacrifices were "so that others could go on".

"It was a combination of imagination and knowledge," he later said. "What Cortez represented to me is the explorer with two sides, one benevolent, the other utterly ruthless."

Typically, he rounds off his version of the story with a final verse about himself, equating his own loss of innocence with the destruction of the Aztec empire.

Despite his questionable historical partisanship, "Cortez The Killer" remains one of Young's towering monuments, a mesmerizing seven-and-a-half-minute guitar epic that has remained a live favourite, cropping up over the years in both electric and acoustic versions.

MONTEZUMA – EMPEROR OF THE AZTECS

THROUGH MY SAILS

When Crosby, Stills, Nash and Young had got together for a working vacation in Hawaii in 1973, hopes were high that the album they planned, to be called *Human Highway*, would top even the achievement of the quartet's multi-platinum *Deja Vu*. Working between Crosby's boat moored in the bay and a beach house they had rented on the island of Maui, Young wrote several new songs for the project, including the title track and "Sailboat Song".

Back in California, they continued to work on the song at Young's ranch before he pulled the plug on the project and went off with Crazy Horse to record *Tonight's The Night*. He later rescued and re-recorded several songs, including "Human Highway" itself, which eventually appeared on 1978's *Comes A Time*.

"Sailboat Song" was the one track to survive in its original form. Renamed "Through My Sails", its alluring simplicity and immaculate CSNY harmonies lend credence to Crosby's claim that *Human Highway* could have been "the best album we ever made."

LONG MAY YOU RUN

The title track from the Stills-Young Band's only album could easily have referred to the long relationship between the record's two main protagonists. However, its true inspiration is revealed in the line "with your chrome heart shinin' in the sun", because Young is actually singing about the 1953 black Pontiac hearse, which he had nicknamed "Mort" and which he had driven from Canada to Los Angeles in March, 1966 on his way to join up with Stills in Buffalo Springfield.

"Long May You Run" is attractive enough, but ultimately as forgettable as you would expect a man singing about an old car to be – although in the liner notes for *Decade* he claims it was written for his "last lady", presumably Carrie Snodgrass. The second verse name-checks the Beach Boys, who, of course, had partly built their career on songs about cars, such as "Fun, Fun, Fun" and "Little Deuce Coup".

"AN ATTEMPT TO WRAP UP SOMETHING THAT WE HAD STARTED A LONG TIME AGO. IT REALLY WASN'T AS HOT AS THE EARLY STUFF WE DID."
YOUNG'S VERDICT ON THE STILLS-YOUNG BAND

MIDNIGHT ON THE BAY

For the Stills-Young album, Young did not call on any of his trusted musicians from Crazy Horse or the Stray Gators but was content to rely on Stills' band, which included percussionists Joe Lala, keyboardist Jerry Aiello, drummer Joe Vitale and George "Chocolate" Perry on bass. They give "Midnight On The Bay" a sophisticated, jazz-lite feel, far smoother than almost any of Young's other records. But, despite its attractive lilt, the song is again slight.

OCEAN GIRL

Young had recently bought two boats, a 100 foot schooner, which he named the *W.N. Ragland*, after maternal grandfather, and another, smaller vessel called *The Evening Coconut*, which earns a namecheck in the "thank yous" on *Long May You Run*. His new-found interest in boats perhaps explains the presence of "Ocean Girl," his second song on the album with a nautical flavour. Yet if singing about his old car on the title track sounded lightweight, his musings on "Ocean Girl" about drinking banana cocktails are total fluff. Even Stills' wah-wah guitar sounds trite.

LET IT SHINE

Young's hostility towards organized religion had already been documented in several songs, so it's hard to regard the country-gospel of "Let It Shine" as anything more than pastiche, particularly given lines such as "I got religion at the airport, my Lord, they caught me waiting for my baggage when I was bored".

More revealing in terms of the nature of Young's own faith is the line when, after asking the Lord to let the light shine, he adds the aside, "although it may not be the only one". This chimes with an interview he gave several years later. "Jesus, Krishna, Buddha. Same story, different imagery," he said. "You could have a religion of the atom."

FOUNTAINBLEAU

Young's one really substantial song on *Long May You Run* was, oddly, inspired by a Miami hotel called the Fountainbleau. His paranoia about Miami Beach, which for him clearly symbolized some hideous vision of the worst of American middle-class culture, had first surfaced in the form of long incoherent monologues about the place in his bizarre *Tonight's The Night* concerts at the end of 1973. In "Fountainbleau", he describes the horror he feels when he finds himself feeling at home among the hotel's clientele of "blue-haired ladies" and elderly patrons in wheelchairs.

AMERICAN STARS 'N BARS/COMES A TIME

AMERICAN STARS 'N BARS

Recorded	December 1974 to April 1977, Nashville, Tennessee; Redwood City, Malibu and Hollywood, California.
Produced by	Neil Young, David Briggs, Tim Mulligan, Elliot Mazer.
Musicians	Neil Young and Crazy Horse with Emmylou Harris, Nicolette Larson and Linda Ronstadt (vocals) and session players.

THE OLD COUNTRY WALTZ; SADDLE UP THE PALAMINO; HEY BABE; HOLD BACK THE TEARS; BITE THE BULLET; STAR OF BETHLEHEM; WILL TO LOVE; LIKE A HURRICANE; HOMEGROWN

COMES A TIME

Recorded	November 1975 to November 1977, Redwood City and Hollywood, California; Nashville, Tennessee; Fort Lauderdale, Florida; London, England.
Produced by	Neil Young, David Briggs, Tim Mulligan, Ben Keith.
Musicians	Neil Young and Crazy Horse with Nicolette Larson (vocals) and session players.

GOIN' BACK; COMES A TIME; LOOK OUT FOR MY LOVE; LOTTA LOVE; PEACE OF MIND; HUMAN HIGHWAY; ALREADY ONE; FIELD OF OPPORTUNITY; MOTORCYCLE MAMA

The art of predicting what Neil Young will do next has never been easy – particularly as he himself has often appeared not to know until the last minute. During the mid-1970s, in particular, he was inclined to plan, record, alter and scrap albums, apparently on a whim. *Tonight's The Night* had been shelved to put out *On The Beach*. Then he had abandoned *Homegrown* in order to resurrect *Tonight's The Night*. Before *Zuma* appeared, he had announced an album called *Ride My Llama*, which never materialized. So it was hardly any surprise that in June 1977, when we had been led to expect an album called *Chrome Dreams*, Young instead chose to release *American Stars 'n Bars*.

He had started to assemble *Chrome Dreams* in late 1976, and, if the subsequent bootleg versions are to be believed, the track listing was "Pocahontas", "Will To Love", "Star Of Bethlehem", "Like A Hurricane", "Too Far Gone", "Hold Back The Tears", "Homegrown", "Captain Kennedy", "Stringman", "Sedan Delivery", "Powderfinger" and "Look Out For My Love". Several of the titles were already familiar to Young aficionados. "Homegrown" had a history and "Star Of Bethlehem" had also been around since 1974. "Pocahontas" and "Powderfinger" had been expected to make the aborted *Ride My Llama* album but eventually turned up on *Rust Never Sleeps*, as did "Sedan Delivery".

"I SOMETIMES REALLY LIKE AGGRAVATING PEOPLE WITH WHAT I DO. I THINK IT'S GOOD FOR THEM."
NEIL YOUNG

Yet when *American Stars 'n Bars* appeared, of the dozen tracks listed for *Chrome Dreams*, only five made the cut, and at least one of them in a radically re-recorded version. As a result, *Chrome Dreams* has come to enjoy almost mythical status, along with *Homegrown*, as one of the great lost Neil Young albums.

"Originally the concept was to have two sides on the album," Young said when asked to explain the changes. "One was going to be American history and the other was going to be social comment. The bar culture kind of thing where I was at the time, you know, drunk on my ass in bars. I couldn't remember the history part, so we left that out."

Having forgotten "the history part", Young instead convened a last-minute session with the faithful Crazy Horse, plus Ben Keith on pedal steel, Carole Mayedo on violin and the backing singers Linda Ronstadt and Nicolette Larson. In a single day at the Broken Arrow ranch they cut an entire side of songs in a loose, country-rock vein, sounding like a boozy, boisterous bar band. Ronstadt and Larson thought it was a rehearsal and were shocked when Young told them they were finished takes. The other side of the vinyl album was a rag bag of earlier songs, taken from sessions for *Homegrown*, *Chrome Dreams* and elsewhere. The resulting album was very uneven.

MEET THE YOUNGS – NEIL AND PEGI HAVE NOW BEEN MARRIED FOR OVER THREE DECADES.

Although "Like A Hurricane" remains one of his best-loved songs, Young again refused to sanction the re-release of *American Stars 'n Bars* for many years – like *On The Beach*, the CD only reappeared in 2003 – fuelling a flourishing bootleg market, where it was sometimes packaged with unreleased tracks purporting to come from the lost albums *Chrome Dreams* and *Homegrown*.

Next up, with a keen sense of his own history, Young released the triple album career retrospective, *Decade*. By the time it appeared in late 1977, he had been fretting over its track-listing for more than a year. In the end, he came up with a highly satisfying selection covering every phase of his career and which included half a dozen songs previously unavailable on album. Intriguingly, it also included a different version of "Long May You Run" – the one with the vocals of Crosby and Nash that were so contentiously wiped from the Stills-Young Band album of the same name. It's appearance was an accident. Young erroneously provided the wrong tape, which he hadn't wiped after all.

By the end of the year, Young was romantically involved with Nicolette Larson and had recorded an album titled *Give To The Wind* with the Gone With The Wind Orchestra, a sprawling supporting cast which included Larson, the Oklahoma guitarist J.J. Cale and more than 20 other musicians. Larson later described the relationship as "like a sponsorship" and by the time the album came out in September 1978 – by then retitled *Comes A*

Time – he had married the pregnant Pegi Morton, who remains his wife to this day. For a brief (and awkward) period, Larson was living in Young's Zuma beach house while Pegi was ensconced at the La Honda ranch.

Comes A Time was not only the accessible, mainstream album that his record company had been wanting him to make ever since *Harvest*. It also became his most commercially successful release in five years, rising to number seven in the *Billboard* lists in America. Not that Young appeared to care. "I like it when people enjoy what I'm doing. But if they don't, I also like it," he said in defence of his contentious output between *Harvest* and *Comes A Time*. "I sometimes really like aggravating people with what I do. I think it's good for them." Two such gentle and melodic records in five year were quite enough, he said – but warned listeners not to expect a third commercial album for at least another five years, when he might relent, "just to convince myself that I can still do it."

NICOLETTE LARSON WOULD ENJOY A TOP TEN CHART HIT IN 1978 WITH YOUNG'S "LOTTA LOVE"

THE OLD COUNTRY WALTZ

With fiddle and pedal steel to the fore and a deliberately hackneyed story line, the opening track of American Stars 'n Bars comes close to a Nashville pastiche. Young's genuine love of country music, the presence of Ronstadt and Larson and the rough, rustic charm save it from toppling totally into the realm of parody. If "The Old Country Waltz" was released today, it would no doubt hailed as an alt-country masterpiece.

Young enjoyed ranch life at La Honda and had an affinity with animals, although he was also heard to complain long and hard about the running costs of maintaining such a large spread. He later wrote a song about his dog Elvis but "Saddle Up The Palomino", another spontaneous country number, name-checks his horse Melody. The song also led to Ronstadt and Larson being given a tongue-in-cheek if not entirely flattering nickname, when Young dubbed them "the Saddle Bags".

LINDA RONSTADT WAS THE BONA FIDE QUEEN OF COUNTRY ROCK IN THE 1970S.

HEY BABE

Another of the songs on the album knocked off in a single session, "Hey Babe" is a forgettable song only made notable by Ben Keith's pedal steel, an instrument that always sounds good on Young's records, because, as the author Peter Doggett perceptively noted, it's the instrument that comes "closest to approaching the lonesome whine of Neil's voice".

HOLD BACK THE TEARS

Described by Merle Haggard as "the best singer I've ever heard", Linda Ronstadt was born in Tucson, Arizona, in 1947. By the mid-1960s she had bought the myth of the Californian dream and moved to Los Angeles. With a great voice that had elements of both country and southern soul, not to mention her smouldering looks, California's rock aristocracy was soon eating out of her hand. After her first band, the Stone Poneys, broke up, she embarked on a solo career, assembling a backing group that would eventually find fame as The Eagles and developing a versatile repertoire that combined contemporary songs by Jackson Browne, Bob Dylan and Young with time-honoured country classics.

Later she moved further into MOR territory, singing standards with the Nelson Riddle orchestra and even having a stab at the light operetta of Gilbert & Sullivan, although she also continued to make fine records in collaboration with Emmylou Harris and Dolly Parton and re-appeared with Young on *Harvest Moon*. When he first called on Ronstadt's services for *American Stars 'n Bars*, she had recently enjoyed big hits with her superb version of "You're No Good" and Hank Williams' "I Can't Help It".

Together with Larson, her backing vocals are at their most powerful on "Hold Back The Tears". The track has something of a Tex-Mex flavour, perhaps enhanced by Ronstadt's own family background, and having grown up close to the Mexican border, where she had learnt all about mariachi music. An earlier version of "Hold Back The Tears" recorded for the aborted *Chrome Dreams* lacks the country inflections but includes additional lyrics.

BITE THE BULLET

The first side of *American Stars 'n Bars* closes with "Bite The Bullet" – with Larson and Ronstadt this time billed as "The Bullets". Lines such as "She's a walking love machine, I like to hear her scream when she bites the bullet" have a frisson of mock danger that matches the untamed raucousness of the recording.

STAR OF BETHLEHEM

By the mid-1970s, Emmylou Harris was emerging as Ronstadt's main rival as the queen of country rock. The springboard for her long career came when her voice was featured to dramatic effect on the two solo albums recorded by Gram Parsons, a former member of the Byrds and the Flying Burrito Brothers, whom Harris had met when she was living in Washington

YOUNG WAS ABLE TO COMMANDEER A STARTLING ARRAY OF FEMALE VOCAL TALENT TO HIS RANKS – SUCH AS THE MAGNIFICENT EMMYLOU HARRIS.

DC and working as a waitress to support her baby daughter. She followed Parsons to LA, and was left devastated when he died of drug-related causes in September 1973.

When Young recruited her to sing on the lovely "Star Of Bethlehem", recorded in Nashville in late 1974, she was about to launch her own solo career. The oldest song on *American Stars 'n Bars*, "Star Of Bethlehem" had been intended for the *Homegrown* album. Years later, by which time Harris was a major star in her own right, Young returned the compliment, by re-recording "Star Of Bethlehem" with her on her 1990 *Duets* album. She also covered Young's "Wrecking Ball" on her 1995 album of the same name, a sublime version that arguably surpassed Young's original.

WILL TO LOVE

"Will To Love", Young defiantly insisted many years later, "might be one of the best records I ever made". Which only goes to prove that artists are not always good judges of their own work. There is something deeply unconvincing about the laborious lyric, which equates a fish struggling to survive in the sea with Young's own flounderings in the ocean of life. Recorded solo and acoustic on a two-track cassette machine, Young enthused about the song to the writer Bill Flanagan in 1990. "I was all alone in my house and I was high on a bunch of things. I was really out there and I wrote the whole thing and put it together. None of the verses are exactly the same length. They're all a little different. I never have sung it, except for that one time."

This isn't strictly true. Young had rehearsed the song for the *Long May You Run* album, but complained that he kept "forgetting what I was doing, losing it totally and getting all pissed off because it didn't sound right."

LIKE A HURRICANE

If ever one song lifted an otherwise ordinary album, it is "Like A Hurricane", one of Young's most ferocious guitar epics, which has remained a live favourite for a quarter of a century.

The song had been premiered live on tour with Crazy Horse in Britain during March 1976. "We'd been trying to record it with two guitars, bass and drums and Neil was kind of giving up on it," recalls Frank Sampedro. "When he started walking out of the studio I played this string instrument and he decided to pick up his guitar. We played it once and at the end of the take he said, 'I think that's the way it goes.' And that's the take on the record."

Young later attempted to describe the song's uniquely hypnotic power in a promotional interview disc for Warner Brothers. "If you listen to that, I never play anything fast," he said. "All it is four notes on the bass. Billy (Talbot) plays a few extra notes now and then, and the drum beat's the same all the way through. It's like a trance we get into. Sometimes it does sound as if we're really playing fast, but we're not. It's just everything starts swimming around in circles."

HOMEGROWN

Young's empathy with farmers would become fully apparent in 1985 when, together with Willie Nelson, he helped organize *Farm Aid*, the first annual star-studded benefit for American farmers. Among those he recruited to perform were Bob Dylan, Emmylou Harris, Joni Mitchell, Roy Orbison, Lou Reed and a host of others. The event raised a reported 10 million dollars and Young has continued to support the cause ever since.

"Homegrown", his tribute to those who work the land, was written more than a decade earlier, and originally composed for the aborted album of the same name. Re-recorded for *American Stars 'n Bars*, the song, of course, not only paid tribute to farmers of a more conventional nature but also those who lived outside the law by growing their own marijuana.

GOIN' BACK

That Young has reverted to something approaching the more pastoral style of *Harvest* on *Comes A Time*, released in September, 1978, is evident from the very first bars of the opening song, "Goin' Back". A gently strummed guitar introduces a warm, high vocal and the strings (by Chuck Cochran) recall Jack Nitzsche's orchestral arrangements for Young's best-selling album, but without the bombast.

"I was going one way and then needed to move in entirely the opposite direction just for some kind of release," Young said in explaining the reversion to a gentler style. "My career is built around a pattern that just keeps repeating itself over and over again."

The song was originally part of an unreleased album that Young conceived as a comic exercise in which he wrote a series of songs using other people's titles. An earlier song called "Goin' Back" had been written by Gerry Goffin and Carole King and recorded by the Byrds and Dusty Springfield, among others. "Little Wing" and "Sail Away" were other borrowed titles in the same series, which would eventually show up on future Young albums.

"I GOT THAT SONG ['LOTTA LOVE'] OFF A TAPE I FOUND LAYING ON THE FLOOR OF NEIL'S CAR."
NICOLETTE LARSON ON THE TRACK THAT WOULD GIVE HER A HIT RECORD

COMES A TIME

The pleasing country lilt of "Comes A Time" has Nicolette Larson harmonizing quite beautifully with Young. Indeed, one can't fail to wonder if they're not thinking about their own briefly blossoming relationship as they sing, "You and I we were captured, we took our souls and we flew away." If so, it was a short-lived flight that was grounded almost before it took wing. The Cajun-country-style fiddle is played by Rufus Thibodeaux, a session player Young first met in Nashville in 1974, who went on to play with him in both the Hawks and Doves band and the International Harvesters.

LOOK OUT FOR MY LOVE

One of only two tracks on *Comes A Time* to feature Crazy Horse, "Look Out For My Love" starts as a gentle acoustic ballad. But you can't keep Talbot, Molina and Sampedro down for long and half way through the song turns semi-electric. According to Sampedro (whom Young nicknamed "Poncho"), the song was recorded in a single night, the group learning the song verse by verse as they went along.

LOTTA LOVE

Born in Montana, Nicolette Larson was 24 when she met Neil Young in April 1977, after Linda Ronstadt had recommended her as a backing vocalist for *American Stars 'n Bars*. Although she had toured with Hoyt Axton and Commander Cody and the Lost Planet Airmen, her pedigree was slight, but she played a substantial role on *Comes A Time*.

She also gave Young the songwriter an unexpected top ten hit single with her version of "Lotta Love." At one stage, Young had planned to include the song on *American Stars 'n Bars*. But by the time he came to release it for *Comes A Time*, Larson had already recorded her own version. "I got that song off a tape I found lying on the floor of Neil's car," she said. "I popped it in the tape player and commented on what a great song it was. Neil said, 'You want it? It's yours.'"

She went on to make half a dozen albums on three different labels between 1978 and 1994, although "Lotta Love" remained her biggest chart success. She also sang on albums by Emmylou Harris and Ronstadt and stayed friendly with Young, singing on both his *Harvest Moon* and *Unplugged* albums. She died tragically of complications arising from cerebral edema in 1997, aged 45.

PEACE OF MIND

Larson is again found harmonizing on the lovely "Peace Of Mind" and in an interview at the time grandiosely likened her partnership with Young to that of the 1930s silver screen heart throbs, Fred Astaire and Ginger Rogers. Her contribution to several of Young's albums – and *Time Out Of Mind* in

particular – was considerable. But when she later referred to *Comes A Time* "wound up being a kind of duet record", it could be argued hat she was perhaps over-stating her role.

YOUNG PLAYED AT THE ILL-FATED ALTAMONT FESTIVAL WITH SCNY WHEN HELL'S ANGELS GANGS BROUGHT A STARK END TO THE DECADE OF PEACE AND LOVE.

HUMAN HIGHWAY

The title song of the "lost" Crosby, Stills, Nash and Young album, "Human Highway" came back into the reckoning for inclusion on *Comes A Time* after Young had revived the title for a film project on which he was concurrently working with his old Topanga neighbour Dean Stockwell.

The Human Highway film eventually saw the light of day in 1982, and saw Young co-directing (under the name Bernard Shakey) and taking the role of Lionel Switch, a mechanic living near a nuclear power station on Earth's final day. It was not well received and Young was forced to concur with the critics. "I know I'm not a great film-maker," he confessed. "If I ever make money on a movie it's going to be by accident."

ALREADY ONE

Young wrote a number of songs about the break-up of his relationship with Carrie Snodgrass. "Already One" is among the most moving, mainly because it centres around their son Zeke, as Young notes that whatever may have become of the relationship between his estranged parents, "our little son won't let us forget". Young was at the time making a great effort to be a responsible father, taking Zeke on the road with him and having him stay for weekends at his La Honda ranch.

FIELD OF OPPORTUNITY

If *Comes A Time* was the belated follow-up to *Harvest*, then "Field Of Opportunity" was the song that made the connection explicit. The reprise "it's plowin' time again" could be read as a blatant reference to his 1972 chart-topping album. But the song also has an acerbic wit that subverts the very idea of a *Harvest* Mark Two. First, Young echoes Dylan's objections to being made the voice of a generation by insisting, "I don't have any answers my friend, just this pile of old questions." Then he mocks the lovelorn troubadour image by singing, "Let me bore you with this story, how my lover let me down."

MOTORCYCLE MAMA

Marianne Faithfull's appearance in the title role of the film *Girl On A Motorcycle* was one of the sexiest images of the 1960s. In America, the film was released under the title *Naked Under Leather*, which was perhaps even more descriptive of the erotic nature of her performance. In addition, the Hell's Angels routinely referred to their girlfriends as "mamas" and the mythic properties of beautiful young women astride shining chrome machines clearly excited Young's imagination. But Young was aware that there was a more sordid reality to the world of bikers, having played the Altamont Festival with CSNY in December 1969, when the violence of the Angel gangs had brought to an end the decade of peace and love in a brutal display of mayhem and murder.

What is most offensive about "Motorcycle Mama", though, is not the Hell's Angels connotation, but the song's crude structure and apparent mindlessness. It may have been meant as a joke, but when it comes to the worst song Young has ever written, "Motorcycle Mama" is a contender.

"Motorcycle Mama" remained neglected until 1993, when surprisingly it began appearing in live set lists. Perhaps Young had been reminded of the earlier song by *Harvest Moon*'s "Unknown Legend", which also contains an idealized image of a woman riding the desert highway on a Harley. Or perhaps he was being characteristically perverse in dredging up a song loathed by so many. Whatever the reason, the song became a concert regular, and in 2000 it was included on the live album *Road Rocks*.

RUST NEVER SLEEPS

Recorded	August 1976 to 1978, Malibu, San Francisco, Redwood City and Hollywood, California; Nashville, Tennessee; Fort Lauderdale, Florida.
Produced by	Neil Young, David Briggs, Tim Mulligan.
Musicians	Neil Young and Crazy Horse: Neil Young (vocals, guitar, harmonica), Billy Talbot (bass, vocals), Ralph Molina (drums), Frank Sampedro (guitar) Additional personnel: Karl T. Himmel (drums), Jo Osborn (bass), Nicolette Larson (backing vocals).

MY MY, HEY HEY (OUT OF THE BLUE)
THRASHER
RIDE MY LLAMA
POCAHONTAS
SAIL AWAY
POWDERFINGER
WELFARE MOTHERS
SEDAN DELIVERY
HEY HEY, MY MY (INTO THE BLACK)

NEIL YOUNG WAS NOT, OF COURSE, A PUNK ROCKER...

The idea of Neil Young as a punk was ludicrous. By the time the Sex Pistols attained their brief notoriety and were threatening to consign rock's bloated "dinosaurs" to the dustbin of musical history, he was a 31-year-old superstar millionaire living on a ranch, not some hungry, street-wise kid getting high on sniffing glue.

Nevertheless, when he first witnessed the gathering punk explosion on a tour of Britain in 1976, Young immediately identified strongly with its ethos. Most of his fellow stars viewed the spotty young punk upstarts with horror. They couldn't sing, they had no proper songs and knew two, or at most three, chords, was the commonly held view among rock's established order.

Young liked punk's energy and its rejection of pomposity and saw in it a reinvention of the original rebel spirit of rock'n'roll. Despite his own wealth, he shared punk's objection to the out-of-touch and pampered lifestyles of many of his increasingly complacent contemporaries. On CSNY's 1974 tour, for example, he had chosen to travel in his own bus because he couldn't stomach the excesses of the circus, which travelled in two private Lear jets and even had customized bed-linen in every hotel sporting a silk-screened logo painted by Joni Mitchell.

In turn, the punks did not dismiss Young as readily as they did most, if not all, of his superstar friends. In many ways, CSNY were an archetype of what punk was reacting against. Yet Young was largely exempt from the strictures of the punks, who recognized in albums such as *Tonight's*

JOHN LYDON, AKA JOHNNY ROTTEN – LEAD SINGER WITH THE SEX PISTOLS AND PUNK ROCK FIGUREHEAD.

The Night a true maverick – someone they could at least respect, even if they couldn't fully identify with him.

Although he wore a Sex Pistols' *Never Mind The Bollocks* t-shirt, the punk revolution at first had little impact on Young's music. By the end of 1977, punk's *annus mirabilis*, he was working on the predominantly acoustic *Comes A Time*, his gentlest record in five years. But a key event occurred in early 1978 when Dean Stockwell, Young's old friend, whose film script had inspired *After The Gold Rush*, told him about the New Wave band Devo who he had seen in a LA club. An intrigued Young checked them out – and promptly invited them to appear in the *Human Highway* film that he and Stockwell were putting together.

During the filming of a private show featuring both Young and Devo at the San Francisco punk club Mabuhay Gardens, the group inadvertently gave him the title of his next album. According to one story, while singing one of Young's new songs, "My My, Hey Hey (Out Of The Blue)", in which he name-checked Johnny Rotten, they jokily began to sing "it's better to burn out because rust never sleeps". Another story holds that Young spotted Mark Mothersbaugh, Devo's synthesizer player, wearing a t-shirt bearing the phrase. It turned out that the "rust never sleeps" slogan had first been invented by two of the band's members when they were working for an advertising agency and were employed on marketing an anti-rust product. Young was much taken with the phrase, which he interpreted as an instruction never to stop moving and always keep changing, to stop your talent from corroding. It was his artistic equivalent of Trotsky's theory of permanent revolution.

"It relates to my career," Young would claim. "The longer I keep on going, the more I have to fight this corrosion. And now that's gotten to be like the World Series for me. The competition's there, whether I will corrode and eventually not be able to move any more and just repeat myself until further notice. Or whether I will be able to expand and keep the corrosion down a little."

Young expanded on his enthusiasm for punk in an LA radio interview. "I don't take it as seriously as before. When you look back at the old bands, they're just not that funny. People want to be funny now. They want to have a good time. That's why the punk thing is so good and healthy. People who make fun of the established rock scene, like Devo and the Ramones, are much more vital to my ears than what's been happening in the last four or five years."

Rust Never Sleeps, released in July 1979, was hardly a punk or even a New Wave album. Side one consisted of all-acoustic songs. But the second, all-electric side, for which Young summoned Crazy Horse once again, was at least influenced by punk's spirit. The result was some of the best reviews Young had received in his career. The British weekly music paper *NME*, which had been punk's most vociferous media cheerleader, called it "the finest album Neil Young has ever released". *NME*'s rival paper, *Sounds*, dubbed the album, "the best Sex Pistols record since 'Pretty Vacant'."

Five months later, Young released a second *Rust* album titled *Live Rust*, recorded at the Cow Palace, San Francisco, in October 1978, which was accompanied by an in-concert film called *Rust Never Sleeps* – again, directed by "Bernard Shakey". The record included in-concert versions of songs on its sister album but, disappointingly, no new material.

MY MY, HEY HEY (OUT OF THE BLUE

Young's immediate response to punk during the summer of 1977 had been to turn his back on rock celebrity by playing incognito in small bars around the Santa Cruz area in California. Hiding under the name The Ducks, the band he assembled included guitarist Jeff Blackburn, whom Young had first known a decade earlier as part of the San Francisco-based duo, Blackburn and Snow. The Ducks were short-lived – when the group's identity became known the attention made it impossible for them to continue playing local bars. Live tapes of the gigs exist in Young's archives. However, they have never been released, leaving "My My, Hey Hey (Out Of The Blue)", on which Blackburn is credited as the co-writer, as the only legacy of this brief but enjoyable escapade.

An acoustic version of the song – recorded live – opens the album and finds Young comparing the death of Elvis Presley ("the king is gone but he's not forgotten") with the rise of Johnny Rotten and the Sex Pistols. Young's new "anti-rust" philosophy is encapsulated in the line "It's better to burn out than to fade away". Several critics seized on the phrase and wondered if Young was glorifying the lengthening list of rock'n'roll casualties. Presley was only 42 when he died. But the tragic roll-call had also claimed many younger victims, including not only his friends Danny Whitten and Bruce Berry but the more substantial talents of Jimi Hendrix, Janis Joplin and Jim Morrison – all needlessly snuffed out long before their powers had begun to "rust".

The line would return to haunt Young in April, 1994, when Kurt Cobain, the troubled lead singer with Seattle grunge pioneers Nirvana, blew his brains out. Near the body was found a suicide note, which quoted the words, "It's better to burn out than to fade away". With horrible irony, Young had at the time been trying to get in touch with Cobain, concerned about reports over Cobain's drug abuse and fragile mental state. He then wrote the song "Sleeps With Angels" about Cobain and his widow, Courtney Love, and pledged he would never again perform "My My, Hey Hey (Out Of The Blue)".

THRASHER

Young's estrangement from his CSNY colleagues was only exacerbated by their diametrically opposed attitudes to punk. David Crosby, in particular, dismissed it contemptuously. In "Thrasher", Young takes a fairly vicious sideswipe at his old colleagues. "There was nothing that they needed, they had nothing left to find," he sings. "So I got bored and left them there, they were just deadweight to me, it's better on the road without that load."

Whatever their artistic differences, the song seems ungracious. Nash certainly had a different perspective and felt that Young had cynically used CSNY to further his solo aspirations. "Neil utilized Crosby, Stills and Nash as a springboard for his own career," he suggested. "It was a very deliberate move and very well done. As soon as CSN didn't suit him he sloughed us off like an old snakeskin."

Young was unrepentant, but later admitted the song had been less than diplomatic. "I felt it was deadweight for me," he insisted to Bill Flanagan in 1990. "I could go somewhere and they couldn't go there. I wasn't going to pull them along, they were doing fine without me."

This was true enough, for the trio's 1977 album *CSN* had reached No. 2 in the American album charts. *Comes A Time* had only reached No. 7 – and that was Young's best chart position in five years.

Relenting a little, he went on to add, "It might have come off a little more harsh than I meant it. But once I write it, I can't say, 'Oh, I'm going to hurt somebody's feelings.'"

RIDE MY LLAMA

First considered as the title song of the album that eventually became *Zuma*, "Ride My Llama" is a strange song about time travel, which involves a Martian, the battle of the Alamo, a journey by llama "from Peru to Texarkana" and ends with Young and his extra-terrestrial friend climbing on board a space ship and smoking dope.

A STATUE OF POCAHONTAS STANDS IN A SMALL ENGLISH CHURCHYARD IN GRAVESEND, KENT.

POCAHONTAS

The Indian princess Pocahontas was the daughter of Powhattan, a sixteenth-century Indian chief. She became a legend after Captain John Smith, one of the early Virginia colonists, was taken prisoner by local Indians in 1607. Powhattan was about to kill him but the captain was saved by the intervention of the 12-year-old Pocahontas. Five years later, she was captured by the colonists and held hostage in Jamestown when one of the settlers, John Rolfe, fell in love with her. She became a Christian, changed her name to Rebecca and married Rolfe. Pocahontas travelled to England in 1616 and was received at the court of James I, but died a year later. She became a national American symbol when Hart Crane gave her a central role in his 1930 poem, *The Bridge*, which Young had read during his visit to London in 1971 and already turned into a song of the same name.

In "Pocahontas", Young details the crimes of the American settlers in massacring the Indian tribes but then jumps to the present day. The final verse moves from "the first tepee" to "the Astrodome" and the action is intriguingly joined by the actor Marlon Brando, a noted campaigner for Native American rights.

SAIL AWAY

Randy Newman had written a song called "Sail Away" about a slave trader, which had included the ironic but controversial line "climb aboard little wog". Young's song was part of a series he wrote as a tongue-in-cheek exercise borrowing other songwriters' titles and which he had played at a series of semi-private concerts which he had filmed in San Francisco for the *Human Highway* movie. With Nicolette Larson on backing vocals, Young's acoustic song picks up the theme of "Pocahontas" in its opening line, "I could live inside a tepee, I could live in Penthouse 35".

POWDERFINGER

On the second side of *Rust Never Sleeps*, Young is reunited with Crazy Horse on "Powderfinger". One of his great narrative songs, it is a frontier tale of a 22-year-old boy fighting unnamed marauders and losing his life in the process.

"Just think of me as one you never figured would fade away so young with so much left undone," Young sings in a line that takes the opposite view to his infamous mantra "it's better to burn out than fade away" on the album's opening song.

A year earlier, Young had offered "Powderfinger" to Lynryd Skynryd, the leading boogie band who had once castigated him in their southern anthem "Sweet Home Alabama". "We sent them an early demo of it because they wanted to do one of my songs," Young recalls. Sadly, fate intervened when singer Ronnie Van Zant and guitarist Steve Gaines were killed in a plane crash in 1977 before they could record the song. However, Young's fellow Canadians the Cowboy Junkies later recorded an excellent cover version.

WELFARE MOTHERS

During 1978, Young had started living in Santa Cruz on the Californian coast, south of San Francisco. "I haven't lived in a town for eight years. I stayed on my ranch in La Honda for about four years and then I just started travelling all over, never really staying anywhere," he explained. "Moving into Santa Cruz is like my re-emergence back into civilization."

There he started improbably hanging out in the local coin-op laundrette, presumably in an attempt to gain an insight into the less privileged side of urban life. "Welfare Mothers" was written after a visit to the laundrette and sleazily suggests that divorcees "make better lovers" with Crazy Horse adding an energetic punk sensibility.

"IT RELATES TO MY CAREER... THE LONGER I KEEP GOING, THE MORE I HAVE TO FIGHT THIS CORROSION." THE ARTIST EXPLAINS THE TITLE OF HIS NEW ALBUM

SEDAN DELIVERY

Many years later, Young denied that *Rust Never Sleeps* had been influenced by punk rock. "Most of the songs on that album had been written well before the Sex Pistols were ever heard of," he insisted. This was partly true because "Sedan Delivery" had first been mooted for inclusion on the abandoned *Chrome Dreams* in 1976. But bootlegs reveal that the earlier version of the song was far slower than the take on *Rust Never Sleeps*, so that even if the writing wasn't influenced by punk, the arrangement certainly was because the song thrashes along at a breakneck speed worthy of The Ramones.

The surreal story moves from playing pool with a woman with varicose veins to a visit to the dentist via an interlude involving Caesar and Cleopatra and a drug deal. The song was revived on the 1997 double live CD with *Crazy Horse, Year Of The Horse*.

HEY HEY, MY MY (INTO THE BLACK)

The album closes with an electric version of the acoustic song that had opened the album. Inexplicably, Jeff Blackburn, who is listed as co-writer on the earlier take, is not given a second credit, even though the song is virtually identical.

HAWKS AND DOVES/ RE-AC-TOR

HAWKS AND DOVES

Recorded	1974 to 1977 and 1980, Nashville, Tennessee; Los Angeles, Malibu, Hollywood, California; Fort Lauderdale, Florida.
Produced by	Neil Young, Tim Mulligan, Elliot Mazer.
Musicians	Neil Young (vocals, guitar, harmonica, piano, vocals), Greg Thomas (drums), Dennis Belfield (bass), Ben Keith (dobro, vocals), Rufus Thibodeaux (fiddle), Ann Hillary O'Brien (vocals), Levon Helm (drums), Tim Drummond (bass), Tom Scribner (saw).

LITTLE WING; THE OLD HOMESTEAD; LOST IN SPACE; CAPTAIN KENNEDY; STAYIN' POWER; COASTLINE; UNION MAN; COMING APART AT EVERY NAIL; HAWKS AND DOVES

RE-AC-TOR

Recorded	October 1980 to July 1981, Redwood City, California.
Produced by	Neil Young, Tim Mulligan, David Briggs, Jerry Napier.
Musicians	Neil Young and Crazy Horse (Neil Young, Frank Sampedro, Billy Talbot, Ralph Molina).

OPERA STAR; SURFER JO AND MO THE SLEAZE; T-BONE; GET BACK; HOME ON ME; SOUTHERN PACIFIC; MOTOR CITY; RAPID TRANSIT; SHOTS

By the start of the 1980s the world was looking an increasingly dangerous place. The idealism of the 1960s was long dead and greed was the new creed. The hippies had given way to the yuppies. The Cold War was approaching a new height and the two superpowers were stockpiling unprecedented quantities of nuclear weapons under a theory of nuclear deterrence that in military circles was, aptly enough, known as MAD (mutually assured destruction).

The election of Ronald Reagan as president at the end of 1980 marked the beginning of a new era of conservatism in which the new leader spouted a bellicose "get tough" policy and denounce the Soviet Union as "the evil empire". Politics was polarizing more than ever into "hawks", who favoured a confrontational approach to the world's rival powers, and the "doves", who favoured a more constructive approach built around dialogue and disarmament treaties. The division was to give Young the title of his first album of the new decade. The only question was – which side was he on?

IN 1978, PEGI YOUNG GAVE BIRTH TO THE COUPLE'S SECOND SON, BEN.

At home Young was facing far more personal battles. In November 1978, his wife Pegi had given birth to his second son, Ben. It swiftly became evident that, like his half-brother Zeke, Ben was suffering from cerebral palsy. "I couldn't believe it. There were two different mothers. It couldn't have happened twice," Young recalled to Jimmy MacDonough, a decade later. The doctors insisted it was a freak coincidence. Yet Young could not help but blame himself.

Worse was to follow when, in March 1980, Pegi was rushed into hospital for an operation on a brain tumour. She was given only a 50/50 chance of survival. She made a complete recovery but Young was shaken and resolved to re-order his priorities and devote himself to ensuring the well-being of his family. "I made up my mind I was going to take care of Pegi, take care of the kids," he explained to MacDonough in an interview for Village Voice. "We were going to go on. We weren't going to be selfish." He told his own father, "I always thought that my music was more important than anything else but now I know that music is important only in that it reflects where I'm at."

Ben was entered on a demanding programme of therapy that involved the boy – and his parents – in lessons and exercises that consumed the entire day. It was "the most difficult thing I've ever done," Young later said. "We had no time to ourselves. Can you imagine what that's like? We couldn't leave the house."

Yet somehow during this traumatic period he managed to find the time to record two albums. *Hawks And Doves*, the first of them, was released in October 1980, and included a number of songs dating from Young's rich catalogue of unreleased material written in the mid-1970s. That could be forgiven under the circumstances, although many found it harder to excuse the right-wing sentiments he appeared to be expressing in some of the newer material. The album failed to make the top 20 in either America or Britain.

"It's what you might call a transitional album for me," Young told Nick Kent many years later, although the phrase could equally be applied to most of his albums over the years. "It's no big thing, just a funky little record that represents where I was at and what I was doing at that time."

Hawks And Doves was recorded without Crazy Horse and with top session men, including the Band's drummer Levon Helm. But by the end of 1980, Young had summoned the group to his ranch to record another album, *Re-ac-tor*. The music had a tough, riff-based repetitive edge but the album sounded almost devoid of emotion. The songs, too, which were virtually all newly written, seemed almost strangulated. In Johnny Rogan's memorable phrase, "the lyrics read like they had been inspired by a car manual." Crazy Horse's Frank Sampedro later described the unsatisfactory way in which the album was recorded. "His mind wasn't focused on the music a lot then. He had other things on his mind. It really shows, I think."

Young does not disagree. "We didn't spend as much time making *Re-ac-tor* as we should've," he confessed to *Mojo* magazine in 1995. The programme with his son Ben was taking up "between 15 and 18 hours of every day." It was "driving, implacable and repetitive," he said at the time. "And so is *Re-ac-tor*."

"JUST A FUNKY LITTLE RECORD THAT REPRESENTS WHERE I WAS AT AND WHAT I WAS DOING AT THAT TIME."
YOUNG RECALLS MAKING *HAWKS AND DOVES*.

Perhaps because of those unhappy associations, *Re-ac-tor* failed to appear on CD until 2003, although the absence of *Hawks And Doves* from his available catalogue until the same time is perhaps harder to explain.

LITTLE WING

That *Hawks And Doves* should open with a song that Young had first recorded for the unreleased *Homegrown* five years earlier is indicative of his creative barrenness as the new decade commenced. Perhaps inspired by Jimi Hendrix's song of the same name, "Little Wing" repeats some of the imagery Young had first used on "Birds" on *After The Gold Rush*.

According to David Crosby, Young offered him the song for his second solo album, which he was trying to record in 1980. By this stage, Crosby was heavily into free-base cocaine and hardly capable of recording. When he handed the record to Capitol, they not only refused to release it but even threatened to send in the bailiffs to repossess his house in an effort to reclaim the advance they had paid him, which he had spent on drugs.

THE OLD HOMESTEAD

Young's ranch at La Honda in northern California had been his main base since he bought it from a pair of lawyers in 1970. By 1980, his family travails meant that he barely left home. It was not surprising, then, that he should revive "The Old Homestead" a song he had written in 1974, and originally considered for inclusion on the aborted *Homegrown* album.

Young claimed the song was an example of "automatic writing". "I wrote 'Homestead' all in one shot, never looking at the previous line until it was finished," he told NME in 1982. "They might be polished a little but they first came through me. I never think 'Oh, I'll write a song with three birds, a guy and a horse in it.'"

A number of critics have suggested that the song is an allegory for Young's relations with Crosby, Stills and Nash. In this interpretation, his old band mates are the three birds who "ditch this rider, shadow and all." If so, it's a case of the author turning the truth on its head, because throughout CSNY's history it has invariably been Young who has ditched his colleagues when it suited him.

LOST IN SPACE

Perhaps inspired by an early TV science-fantasy series of the same name, "Lost In Space" finds Young on the sea bed, and uses similarly child-like sub-aquatic imagery to that deployed by the Beatles in "Octopus's Garden" on Abbey Road.

CAPTAIN KENNEDY

The first side of *Hawks And Doves* ends with yet another old song that predated 1977's *American Stars 'n Bars*. One of Young's more notable narrative compositions, "Captain Kennedy" tells the story of a World War Two naval commander who loses his ship in action. After the war, he saves enough money to go back to sea in a wooden schooner.

The tale is related through the eyes of the captain's son, which raises the obvious question over whether the song is autobiographical. In fact, there is only a tangential relationship between Captain Kennedy's war record and that of Young's own father, Scott, who enlisted as a seaman in 1943 and spent most of the rest of the war in Europe. Neil was born in November 1945, after the war had ended. He was, nevertheless, a "war baby", conceived while his father was on leave in Toronto, before being posted to the Pacific. In the event, the atom bombs dropped on Hiroshima and Nagasaki in August 1945 bought the war to a swifter conclusion than anticipated, and Scott Young never got to see action in the Pacific.

STAYIN' POWER

Like *American Stars 'n Bars*, Young conceived *Hawks And Doves* as two distinct and contrasting halves. The second, country-influenced side opens with "Stayin' Power", which sounds like a celebration of the old-fashioned "family values" being championed by the newly-triumphant Reaganite right. Yet Young can surely be forgiven such sentiments given the duress his own family was under. The line "I ain't leaving, no way" is a heartfelt pledge to Ben and Pegi – and perhaps one that he needed to make because it was only a few years earlier that he had left Carrie Snodgrass and his first son, Zeke.

COASTLINE

Another hearty country romp, "Coastline" repeats the themes of perseverance in the face of adversity that are explored in "Stayin' Power". The celebration of the hard-working ethic of the all-American male is again given a personal twist as Young relates it to his own family circumstances. The line "we don't back down from no trouble" summarizes his attitude when confronted with Ben's illness, although it also coincidentally reflected the Reagan administration's attitude to global politics.

UNION MAN

"I really like 'Union Man'," Young told the British journalist Nick Kent in 1995. It was an odd track for him to single out for praise, for politically it is one of the least attractive songs on *Hawks And Doves*, as Young gratuitously attacks the Musicians Union and satirizes its members and their concerns. At the time, the union was leading an entirely laudable campaign "to keep music live", so you wonder what they ever did to upset the millionaire superstar.

Perhaps his anti-union sentiments had been festering since the *Time Fades Away* tour with the Stray Gators in 1973. Observing that everywhere they played, Young was breaking box-office records, his hired musicians ganged up half way through the tour to demand a pay rise. A furious Young refused their demands and the rest of the tour was conducted amid considerable rancour and bitterness.

COMING APART AT EVERY NAIL

Having dissed trade unions in the previous song, "Coming Apart At Every Nail" finds Young posing as the friend and champion of the unassuming hard-working "ordinary Joe". The song deplores the cracks in the fabric of American society yet is hardly written from a radical perspective. Its patriotic assertions have more in common with the hackneyed, flag-waving conventions of redneck country songs. The track is lifted by the spirited backing vocals of Ann Hillary O'Brien, who takes over the role previously filled by Linda Ronstadt and Nicolette Larson.

RONALD REAGAN, THE 40TH PRESIDENT OF THE UNITED STATES OF AMERICA – AND THE FACE OF 1980S CONSERVATISM.

HAWKS AND DOVES

Four years after the release of *Hawks And Doves*, Bruce Springsteen's song "Born In The USA" would be praised by Ronald Reagan as a patriotic, all-American anthem. Typically, he missed Springsteen's sense of irony and the songwriter was irked that his words should be so misunderstood. Yet Neil Young had been there first. "I ain't tongue-tied, just don't got nothing to say, I'm proud to be living in the USA," he sang on the title track of *Hawks And Doves* – and the critics have been arguing over how serious his jingoism is ever since.

Young's defenders claim that he was satirizing mindless patriotism and the song is an example of "method acting". He's not even American but Canadian, they point out. Others have cited further reactionary sentiments he was to express later in the decade as evidence that he was in earnest. Characteristically, Young himself is ambiguous about his true intention. "There is a character in there, but he reflects a lot of the ways that I have felt," he admitted to Bill Flanagan in 1990. "It's not really like me, but it is. I can hide behind it. I can say things through somebody else that I couldn't say myself."

OPERA STAR

The idea behind the opening song on *Re-ac-tor* could have been interesting. The story of a rock'n'roller who loses his girlfriend to an opera lover could have been the springboard for all kinds of fascinating observations on cultural conflicts and the nature of "high" and "low" art. Yet like so much else on the album, "Opera Star" is under-developed and suggests a rushed album into which insufficient thought has gone.

SURFER JO AND MO THE SLEAZE

Despite being signed to the biggest corporate label in America, Young has retained a feisty and independent credibility as someone who refuses to play by the cash-driven rules of the record industry "suits". The characters in "Surfer Joe" and "Mo The Sleaze" are reputedly Joe Smith and Mo Ostin, the two senior executives with Warners/Reprise. The song is a private joke in which he entices the pair on a pleasure cruise with the promise of "plenty of women, plenty of booze." It's a put-down, but a good-natured one.

Ostin, a soberly dressed family man who wore thick-rimmed glasses, had been hired by Frank Sinatra to run Reprise in 1961. Despite an instruction from Sinatra never to sign a rock'n'roll band, within two years Ostin had signed the Kinks and the floodgates were open. Smith, a smooth talker and the more flamboyant of the two, became Ostin's deputy after he had been put in charge of Warner's as well as Reprise. Smith later succeeded David Geffen as head of Elektra/Asylum.

Young was particularly close to Ostin and years later thanked him by name in his acceptance speech when he was inducted into the Rock'n'Roll Hall Of Fame. When Ostin was ousted as chairman in 1995, Young considered quitting the label. The unhappy memory of his brief spell away from Warners/Reprise in the 1980s when he signed with David Geffen may well have been the chief factor in dissuading him from going through with his threatened walk out.

T-BONE

Arguably the most turgid performance in Young's recorded canon, "T-Bone" consists of nine minutes of utter tedium stuck in a single groove with the endlessly repetitive lyric, "Got mashed potatoes, ain't got no t-bone." With typical perversity, Young later insisted that he considered the song – if it can be so called – to be the best track on *Re-ac-tor.* "The night we recorded that we didn't have anything else happening," he recalled. "I just made up the lyrics and we did the whole thing that night. It was a one-take thing. It seems the lyrics were just on my mind. It's very repetitive but I'm not such an inventive guy. I thought those two lines were good."

Perhaps the sheer mindlessness of the song was a welcome release from the demanding regime he was following all day with his son Ben. Whatever the circumstances behind the late-night recording, it barely deserved any kind of commercial release.

GET BACK HOME ON ME

Re-ac-tor continues on its pointless course with a nondescript slice of R&B and apparently meaningless references to General Custer and Robert E. Lee, although the song has nothing to do with the American Civil War. "Get Back Home On Me" is at least an improvement on "T-Bone", which precedes it, but only because mercifully it's shorter.

SOUTHERN PACIFIC

One of the album's better songs, "Southern Pacific" expresses Young's love of trains and tells the story of an old railway engineer, Casey Jones, who also features in the traditional American folk song, "The Ballad of Casey Jones," and a Grateful Dead song on their 1970 album *Workingman's Dead*.

Young's passions for trains also led him around this time to build a 4,000 square feet model railway for his sons in a barn on his ranch. Several

AN UNLIKELY TRAIN FANATIC, YOUNG EVEN BOUGHT HIS OWN MODEL RAILWAY COMPANY.

years later he pursued his obsession even further when he bought the model railway company Lionel Trains.

MOTOR CITY

Ever since his famous hearse "Mort" had brought him from Canada to LA in 1966, Young had loved cars almost as much as he loved trains. By the mid-1970s he was a collector of classic and vintage models. But by the start of the 1980s, Detroit – which as the centre of the American automobile industry had been known as the "motor city" for decades – was feeling the squeeze and laying off workers. In particular, Japanese models such as Mitsubishi and Nissan were starting to make a serious dent in the American market, hence Young's gratuitous jibe at Japanese cars in "Motor City", a song in which he expresses a preference for a good old American Jeep.

RAPID TRANSIT

The most famous stutter in rock belongs to Roger Daltrey on The Who's "My Generation". Young attempts something similar on "Rapid Transit." The punkish, choppy backing from Crazy Horse sounds like a second-rate Talking Heads and having only a year or two earlier championed punk and new wave, here Young's lyric seems to be taking a swipe at it.

SHOTS

Young had unveiled "Shots", the oldest song on the album, in early 1978 when he had essayed a solo acoustic version at the Boarding House in San Francisco as part of a set that was filmed for *Human Highway*. Its lyric deals with the generation gap through an image of children on the beach attempting to restore the crumbling sand castles built by their fathers. After the banalities of songs such as "T-Bone" the words appear sophisticated and thoughtful, although in keeping with *Re-ac-tor*'s blank emotional radar, Young and Crazy Horse smother the song in noise and feedback so that its subtleties are semi-concealed. Nevertheless, it's the most intense performance on the record, although those familiar with both versions tend to prefer the more poetic style of the earlier acoustic rendition.

TRANS

Recorded	September 1981 to May 1982, Redwood City, California; Honolulu, Hawaii.
Produced by	Neil Young, Tim Mulligan, David Briggs.
Musicians	Neil Young and Crazy Horse: Neil Young (vocals, guitar, bass, synclavier, vocoder, electric piano), Ralph Molina (drums, vocals), Frank Sampedro (guitar, stringman), Billy Talbot (bass). Additional personnel: Nils Lofgren (guitar, piano, organ, electric piano, synclavier, vocals), Ben Keith (pedal steel guitar, slide guitar, vocals), Bruce Palmer (bass), Joe Lala (percussion, vocals)

LITTLE THING CALLED LOVE
COMPUTER AGE
WE R IN CONTROL
TRANSFORMER MAN
COMPUTER COWBOY (AKA SYSCRUSHER)
HOLD ON TO YOUR LOVE
SAMPLE AND HOLD
MR SOUL
LIKE AN INCA

YOUNG'S SHIFT TOWARD ELECTRONIC MUSIC CAME AS A SURPRISE TO HIS NEW LABEL.

Neil Young's departure from Reprise after a dozen years as a solo artist with the label was to prove to be one of the most fateful of his career. At first it had looked as if Young would sign with RCA, who came up with a seven-album offer that his manager Elliott Roberts calculated was worth nine million dollars. Then, at the eleventh hour, David Geffen joined the race with a counter offer and snatched Young away with all kinds of promises that it turned out he had little intention of keeping.

But did Young jump or was he pushed? According to Geffen's authoritative biographer Tom King, the idea that Young should sign with the newly-founded Geffen Records was first floated by Mo Ostin, the head of Warners/Reprise. Ostin was instrumental in Geffen's decision to set up the label and had been the one who suggested to the former Asylum Records boss that he should re-enter the record industry in a joint-venture company in which Warner's would take a fifty per cent stake. Possibly Ostin was already resigned to Young leaving Reprise and merely wanted to scotch the RCA contract. But as an inducement to closing the joint-venture deal with Geffen, King reports that Ostin volunteered a transfer deal involving Young as the star artist whom the new label required to facilitate its launch.

Young knew Geffen well, because his new record label boss had formerly co-managed CSNY with Elliott Roberts. The notoriously volatile Geffen had remained on friendly terms with Roberts, who had continued to manage Young's solo career and so the deal was easily brokered. Young was assured by both his own manager and Geffen that the new label would offer him total artistic control. "David has worked with Neil for a very long time," Roberts reminded the British-based Young fanzine *Broken Arrow*. "He totally relates to Neil as an artist and he has no preconceived notions about Neil. He knows he's capable of doing anything at any point at any time." He went on to add that Young's unpredictability meant that his albums were "not always commercial from the record company's point of view". But, he insisted, Geffen "relates to that".

Roberts' words soon came back to haunt him. Young took off to Hawaii – almost the first time he had left his ranch in more than two years – and recorded a batch of acoustic songs with Crazy Horse bassist Ralph Molina and percussionist Joe Lala, which he presented to Geffen as the basis for an album to be called *Island In The Sun*. His new record company boss did not like what he heard and felt the songs were insubstantial. "They advised me not to put it out," a still pissed-off Young complained to *Rolling Stone* in 1988. "It was a tropical thing all about sailing, ancient civilizations, islands and water," he told *Mojo* seven years later.

DAVID GEFFEN'S CLAIMED ACCEPTANCE OF NEIL YOUNG'S UNPREDICTABILITY WOULD SOON BE SEVERELY TESTED.

Yet at the time Young does not appear to have fought Geffen particularly hard over the proposed record, and the truth was that he wasn't sure himself that his heart was in another predominantly acoustic album. By now his head was full of a fascination with electronic techno music of the kind purveyed by the experimental German group Kraftwerk.

Having only recently been extolling the back-to-basics simplicities of punk, Young now embraced the full panoply of electro-pop – drum machines, sequenced synthesizers, tape loops and, above all, the vocoder, a device that altered the sound of the human voice to resemble a machine or, as Sylvie Simmons bluntly puts it in her monograph, "a robot dog".

Young was not alone in his infatuation with the Kraftwerk model. British groups such as Human League, Cabaret Voltaire, Depeche Mode as well as David Bowie and Gary Numan had already fallen under the group's techno spell. In fact, Young was something of a late arrival at the electronic feast, because the record that alerted him to the possibilities of electro-pop, 1981's *Computer World*, was the eighth album of Kraftwerk's career.

Young was hooked and turned back to the group's 1977 recording, *Trans-Europe Express*, to give him the title of his next album. In the summer of 1982, he also put together a band of old friends he dubbed the Trans-Band and took them off for a tour of Europe, partly because European fans had missed out on his previous tour and partly because the idea of playing his new experimental music in its birthplace appealed to him.

It was a costly undertaking and when the budget ran out of control, Young dropped the Trans-Band – which included Nils Lofgren, Ben Keith, Ralph Molina, Joe Lala and Bruce Palmer from Buffalo Springfield – and on American dates appeared alone with a computer and duetted with his own image on a giant backdrop screen.

The *Trans* album was released in January, 1983. "I feel that with the new digital and computerized equipment I can get my hands on now, I can do things I could never do before. I've always loved machines. If you don't experiment you're dead," Young said on its release. Young's faith in technology also caused him, around the same time, to decline to join the anti-nuclear power benefit concerts organized by MUSE (Musicians United for Safe Energy) to which CSN, Jackson Browne, Tom Petty, Bruce Springsteen, James Taylor and others enthusiastically lent their support. "To refuse nuclear energy today is like preferring the horse to the car," Young told them somewhat pompously.

But there was another agenda at work behind *Trans*, which had little to do with Young the modernist technocrat. He and Pegi had taken Ben out of the harsh physical programme that had proved so demanding but produced few tangible results. Instead they had enrolled their son in a new therapy endorsed by the National Academy for Child Development, which concentrated on developing communication skills in the still non-speaking child. In this context, the vocoder was an obvious device to try.

Young later described *Trans* as "an incredibly personal record, maybe the most personal thing I've ever done." He went on to elaborate in emotional terms: "*Trans* is about communication, about not getting through. And that's what my son is. You gotta realize you can't understand the words on *Trans* and I can't understand my son's words. So feel that."

"*Trans* was obviously very important to him," recalls journalist Allan Jones, who interviewed Young for *Melody Maker* at the time. "Even years later he'd still get really animated talking about it." Although Trans made the top 20 in America and the top 30 in Britain (a better showing than either *Hawks And Doves* or *Re-ac-tor*), many of his long-term fans remained baffled. Even Nick Kent, one of Young's most perceptive critics, made no concession to the circumstances behind its recording and dismissed the record as "an unintelligible sci-fi rock opera about computers" that "made no sense to anyone".

LITTLE THING CALLED LOVE

The opening track of *Trans* sounds like "classic" Neil Young. As such it is utterly misleading and gives no hint of the futuristic experiments to come. One of the songs on the proposed *Island In The Sun* that had been unceremoniously rejected, the re-recorded version of "Little Thing Called Love" rocks with old-fashioned abandon and features an irresistibly catchy chorus. The lyrics may be slight but at least without the vocoder they're decipherable. But anyone who bought *Trans* believing that the opening song was representative of the album would have been perfectly justified in asking for their money back.

COMPUTER AGE

As someone who had famously come to rely on instinct rather than technique when recording, Young shocked most of his fans by kicking off on "Computer Age" with a drum machine and an electro-pop synthesizer. The vocoder, basically a device for dehumanizing the human voice, was an even more extraordinary technological innovation for Young to embrace.

In part, he was deliberately undermining the image of the sensitive singer-songwriter. "All the soul and feeling we're talking about," he told David Gans immediately before the release of *Trans*, "it has nothing to do with reality. Reality is in cubicles and digital blocks." Oscar Wilde had a famous saying about consistency being "the hobgoblin of a small mind". It was just one of many occasions in Young's career when he proved an enthusiastic advocate of Wilde's aphorism.

"Computer Age" paints a futuristic picture of a machine-dominated world that blurs the distinction between flesh and blood and the purely mechanical. The song was meant to be accompanied by a video (which was never made) featuring families rushing to a hospital but getting trapped in a nightmare traffic jam.

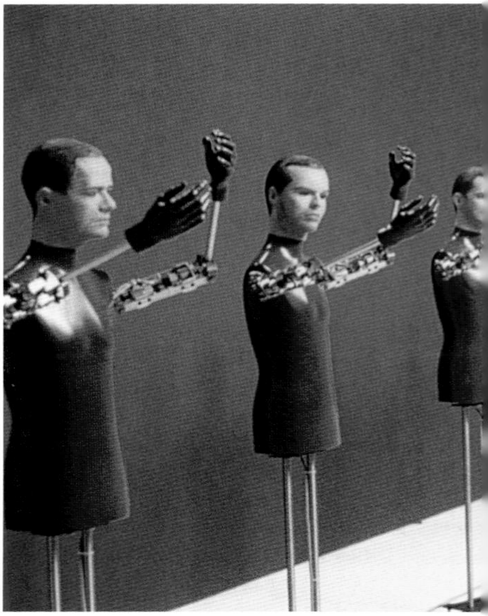

IN SPITE OF RELATIVELY MODEST COMMERCIAL SUCCESS, KRAFTWERK ARE AMONG THE MOST INFLUENTIAL BANDS OF THE PAST FOUR DECADES.

"Watching the lights change, their eyes start to be like traffic lights," Young said in 1992. In the song he appears to find some comfort in the computer's negation of humanity, although the sentiment doesn't last. "I need you to let me know that there's a heartbeat," he declares in the last verse which, in retrospect, sounds like a desperate expression of his attempts to communicate with his non-verbal son. He attempted to explain his emotional dilemma in 1990. "You can only feel so much, then you have to deny it," he said. "There are going to be times when you want to disguise yourself and not let everything out. Some things are too painful and shouldn't be let out. But they have to come out anyway."

WE R IN CONTROL

The dystopian vision of "Computer Age" is taken even further in "We R In Control", a Devo-influenced song in which the machines have finally taken over. Young's vocoder-disguised voice intones the song's title in what might have been a nightmarish glimpse of the future along the lines of George Orwell's *1984* or Aldous Huxley's *Brave New World* but instead comes over as merely irritating and faintly risible.

TRANSFORMER MAN

The new programme that Ben Young was now following relied on technology for the speechless boy to communicate with his parents and the outside world. In this context, "Transformer Man" becomes a moving tribute to Young's son and his speech difficulty. The "push of a button" is the technology that allows him to express himself, and which turns the boy into the "transformer man" with "power in your hand". Again, with the benefit of hindsight, lines such as "unlock the secrets, let us throw off the chains that hold you down" are full of an almost unfathomable heartache. At the time, because Young kept his own counsel, they seemed merely part of a banal vision of some ridiculously idealistic robot-run world.

The format in which Young's normal voice is then answered by incomprehensible vocoder replies also makes more sense in the knowledge of Ben's circumstances. "That was the point I was making, how difficult and painful it can be to communicate, which is something we often just take for granted," Young told *Melody Maker*.

COMPUTER COWBOY (AKA SYSCRUSHER)

Young's imagination is at its most bizarre on "Computer Cowboy", which begins as if it's a comment on factory farming in which "the cattle each have numbers and they all eat in a line". But Young's techno-minded cowboy is a Jekyll and Hyde character with another life. He "rides the range to midnight" as Young's distorted voice chants a machine-inspired version of the old cowboy call, "cow cow yippie, yippie-ay". Then he turns into an anarchist cyber-terrorist, the "syscrusher" (system-crusher) who rides into the city and breaks into office buildings to crash the computer systems of corporate America.

"During the day he was a cowboy," Young explained in 1992. "All his cows were the same. They were digital cows, square block cows. He had a floodlight out on the pasture that he kept alight all night, so there were 24 hours of light for the cows to be eating and moving towards their final goal, the perfect cattle ranch. But at night when he turned on the lights, he'd go into the city and start fucking around with the computers of companies. He'd go inside buildings, fuck up the memory systems and the government records."

HOLD ON TO YOUR LOVE

The second song to be rescued from the scrapped *Island In The Sun* album, "Hold On To Your Love", is given a makeover with a synth-pop sound to make it seem less out of place with the album's techno-theme. But it's sung in Young's human voice and the lyrics with their simplistic love-will-save-the-day message are so lightweight that it's hard to understand quite what it's doing there.

SAMPLE AND HOLD

By 1983, genetic cloning and Dolly the Sheep were still some years off but futurists were already seriously speculating about the possibility of DNA manipulation to produce perfect neo-human specimens. In "Sample and Hold" Young may be considers the possibility and jokes about a robotic computer dating service in an amusing lyric about the creation of a "unit" that is "perfection in every detail, fabricated from the curl of the hair to the tip of the nail."

MR SOUL

The former Buffalo Springfield bass player Bruce Palmer, who had accompanied Young on his journey by hearse from Canada to LA in 1966, had suddenly reappeared in Young's world in 1982. The two had seen very little of each other since the mid-1970s but Palmer had got in touch to suggest a Springfield reunion. It never happened but Young was pleased enough to see his old friend and invited him to Hawaii to rehearse with the Trans Band.

Palmer subsequently toured and recorded with Young in 1982–83, and perhaps it was his presence that persuaded Young to revive "Mr Soul" from *Buffalo Springfield Again*. If so, it was a move designed to provoke even Young's most loyal fans as his voice is mangled by the vocoder and the song is given a sledgehammer disco beat.

"AN INCREDIBLY PERSONAL RECORD, MAYBE THE MOST PERSONAL THING I'VE EVER DONE."
YOUNG'S VIEW OF *TRANS*

LIKE AN INCA

Young's interest in the Aztec and Inca civilisations was first expressed on 1975's *Zuma* in "Cortez The Killer" when he had even contemplated an entire album around the theme of time travel and ancient civilizations. Several other songs explored the theme further on subsequent albums and "Like An Inca" stands in this tradition.

Lyrically, the song's imagery is intriguing with powerful references to a condor, a praying mantis, a gypsy fortune-teller and a sacred altar. A verse about the threat of nuclear destruction also finds Young singing with a passion he barely musters elsewhere on the album. "Like An Inca" also contains the record's best guitar playing and to many it is the undisputed highlight of the album. The tune was in part borrowed from a mid-1970s song called "Hitchhiker", which Young later resurrected as a solo piece in concert in 1992. But the dull and repetitious groove of the version recorded for *Trans* means the track is never more than a distant cousin of such guitar epics as "Cortez The Killer" and "Like A Hurricane" and fails to match their dynamic force.

EVERYBODY'S ROCKIN'

After the electro-pop of *Trans*, Young next decided to go back to basics with an album of country songs, under the working title *Nashville Album* but subsequently retitled *Old Ways*. For the second time, Geffen refused to release the album that Young delivered him and demanded something "more rock'n'roll".

An infuriated Young decided to take him at his word and delivered instead a pure rockabilly album that remains the shallowest of his entire career. Credited to "Neil and The Shocking Pinks", the album cover depicted him in an Elvis pose wearing white suit, pink tie and back shirt and with slicked back hair. Inside lay an even greater shock. Four of *Everybody's Rockin's* ten songs were covers and the entire record unforgivably contained less than 25 minutes of music. In truth, the album warrants very little in the way of in-depth coverage – indeed, most Neil Young fans would consider it best forgotten.

The songs he chose to cover – Bobby Freeman's "Betty Lou's Got A Brand New Pair Of Shoes", Jimmy Reed's "Bright Lights Big City", Elvis Presley's "Mystery Train" and "Rainin' In My Heart" – were indeed fine tracks in their original 1950s recordings. Neither is there any doubt that in his youth Young had genuinely loved the music of the era. However, his versions on *Everybody's Rockin'*, and the cliché-ridden new compositions he wrote in imitation of the style, come over as parody and pastiche rather than loving tribute.

Young's own view of the record came across as confused and contradictory. "What am I? Stupid?" he demanded rhetorically when Kent pressed him. "Did people really think I put that out thinking it was the greatest fuckin' thing I'd ever recorded? Obviously I'm aware it's not." Then he insisted *Everybody's Rockin'* was another of his attempts to keep the corrosion at bay by consistently wrong-footing his audience. "It was a way of further destroying what I'd already set up. Without doing that, I wouldn't be able to do what I'm doing now," he said. "If I build something up, I have to systematically tear it right down before people decide, 'Oh, that's how we define him.'"

As a justification it rings hollow. But if it was an exercise in destroying what he'd set up, then *Everybody's Rockin'* was an absolute triumph. The album failed to make the top 40 in either Britain or America and, by the end of the year, Geffen had taken out an unprecedented law suit against

Young in an LA court seeking three million dollars compensation and damages for providing albums that "were not commercial in nature" and "musically uncharacteristic" of his previous records.

For the sake of completion, here is a brief glimpse at the "original" compositions on *Everybody's Rockin'*.

"**Payola Blues**", co-written with Ben Keith is the best of the new tracks. Dedicated to the 1950s disc jockey Alan Freed, it compares the corruption of backhanders to get records on the radio in the 1950s with the radio plugging of a later day. The reference to giving away a new Mercedes Benz to get the record on the radio became almost a self-fulfilling prophesy when Geffen Records bought an old Cadillac to give away in a radio contest to promote the record.

"**Wonderin'**" was an old song Young had first recorded as a demo in 1969 and discarded as too insubstantial. The Jerry Lee Lewis-influenced "**Kinda Fonda Wonda**" is equally lightweight, although there is mild amusement to be found in the way the lyric name drops a series of classic 1950s songs that incorporated girls names, including "Run Around Sue" and "Long Tall Sally".

"**Jellyroll Man**" is instantly forgettable. "**Cry Cry Cry**" features an unconvincing doo wop chorus and a ridiculous "boo hoo hoo" refrain from Young but is partly redeemed by some decent guitar from Ben Keith. The title track, "**Everybody's Rockin'**", concludes an album that lacks any significant highs with yet another low.

Young later complained that Geffen had excluded two songs, "Get Gone" and "Don't Take Your Love Away From Me", from the planned tracklisting and claimed they "would've given it a lot more depth". Both were eventually released in 1993 on *Lucky Thirteen* in live versions recorded a decade earlier. Although the Shocking Pinks sound more convincing as a live band and the tracks would have made *Everybody's Rockin'* better value for money by pushing the music over the half hour mark, the songs are nonetheless insubstantial.

Young would later claim that *Everybody's Rockin'* was indeed an act of revenge, and that he had given Geffen the album "vindictively". And yet a dozen years after it was released, Young was still boasting to Nick Kent in *Mojo* that *Everybody's Rockin'* was "as good as *Tonight's The Night* as far as I'm concerned." Whilst going on to admit that there was "very little depth" to the material, he ardently insisted, "There was a time when all music was like that, when all pop stars were like that. And it was good music, really good music."

OLD WAYS

Recorded	January 1983 to April 1985, Nashville and Franklin, Tennessee; Spicewood and Austin, Texas.
Produced by	Neil Young, David Briggs, Ben Keith and Elliot Mazer.
Musicians	Neil Young (vocals, guitar, banjo-guitar, harmonica), Waylon Jennings (guitar, vocal), Willie Nelson (guitar, vocal), Rufus Thibodeaux (fiddle), Ben Keith (pedal steel guitar, dobro), Tim Drummond (bass), Karl Himmel (drums), Joe Allen (bass), Ralph Mooney (pedal steel guitar), Hargus "Pig" Robbins (piano), Gordon Terry (fiddle), Joe Osborn (bass), Anthony Crawford (mandolin, vocal), Terry McMillan (harmonica, Jew's harp), Béla Fleck (banjo), Bobby Thompson (banjo), David Kirby (guitar), Grant Boatwright (guitar), Johnny Christopher (guitar), Ray Edenton (guitar), Gove Scrivenor (autoharp), Farrell Morris (percussion), Marty Stuart (mandolin), Carl Gorodetzky (violin), Spooner Oldham (piano), Larry Byrom, Rick Palombi, Doana Cooper, Denise Draper, Gail Davies, Betsy Hammer, Pam Rose, Janis Oliver-Gill, Mary Ann Kennedy, Kristine Oliver-Arnold, Leona Williams (vocals).

THE WAYWARD; GET BACK TO THE COUNTRY; ARE THERE ANY MORE REAL COWBOYS?; ONCE AN ANGEL; MISFITS; CALIFORNIA SUNSET; OLD WAYS; MY BOY; BOUND FOR GLORY; WHERE IS THE HIGHWAY TONIGHT?

"I FOUGHT WITH HIM BECAUSE I WANTED HIM TO DO BETTER WORK. BECAUSE I LOVE HIM."
DAVID GEFFEN TRIES TO JUSTIFY HIS LAW SUIT

After *Everybody's Rockin'*, Young decided to resurrect the concept of the country record he had originally called *Nashville Album* but which later came to be known as *Old Ways*. That Geffen should have objected to his wishes to release a country record is on the surface strange, given that *Nashville* was where much of *Harvest*, his best-selling album, had been recorded. But by now Geffen had lost all patience with Young. His star artist had given him an electronic album and a rockabilly record and was now hell bent on releasing another genre experiment when all Geffen wanted was for him to make another rock'n'roll record like *Rust Never Sleeps*, his last major seller.

Geffen began to believe that Young was deliberately taking him for a ride and told Roberts that Geffen Records would not release any further money to Young unless he agreed to hire a producer for his next record selected, or at least approved, by Geffen himself. Not surprisingly, Roberts and Young refused and Geffen brought matters to a head by instructing his attorney Eric Eisner to stop authorizing payment of Young's studio costs. Soon Young found himself in the humiliating position of turning up at a New York studio booked in his name only to find the doors barred. "You guys are fucking me," Geffen screamed at his old friend Elliott Roberts, when Young's manager protested. Young and Roberts decided to ignore Geffen's rantings and ravings and carried on recording at their own expense.

Geffen responded by filing a suit against Young on November 4, 1983, accusing him of fraud and deceit, alleging he had broken promises to deliver commercial albums and seeking damages in excess of three million dollars. It was a ludicrous action, which Geffen never had the remotest chance of winning.

Young's own lawyers swiftly issued a countersuit, alleging breach of contract and fraud and seeking even higher compensation and damages than Geffen was demanding. Young was also determined to press on with *Old Ways*. Indeed, Geffen's behaviour brought out his stubborn streak and made him even more intransigent. "The more everybody said 'don't do this', the more I realized I must be doing the right thing. Whenever I try to do something different everybody tells me not to do it," he told the *Boston Globe*. "I told them, 'the longer you sue me for playing country music, the longer I'm going to play country music'. Either you back off or I'm going to play country music for ever."

Yet he admitted to Geffen's biographer Tom King in 1998 that he was shaken by the turn of events. He also confided that if he had come up with another surefire hit song like "Heart Of Gold" or even "Lotta Love", he had planned to sit on it until he was off Geffen's label. There was "no fucking way" he was going "to deliver the mother lode to those guys," he told King.

Meanwhile, he assembled a crack country band dubbed the International Harvesters featuring pedal steel, fiddle and banjo and carried on recording. By the time *Old Ways* was eventually released in August 1985, some two years after *Everybody's Rockin'*, Geffen had realized he had launched a suit he couldn't win and the action was quietly dropped. The settlement decreed that Young would fulfil his five-album obligation to Geffen Records but the record company would finally allow Young the artistic control he believed he had been guaranteed in the first place. "Geffen's being good about it now. They're letting me do what I want to do," Young told an American journalist, even more remarkably claiming, "They're my friends now." The terms of the settlement required both parties to display civility in their public pronouncements and Geffen in turn insisted, "I fought with him because I wanted him to do better work. Because I love him." Some years later there was a more genuine rapprochement after Geffen admitted in a magazine interview that he "regretted" suing Young.

Although the public generally sided with Young in the legal dispute, they nonetheless appeared to agree with Geffen about the uncommerciality of Young's genre-hopping oeuvre. *Old Ways* failed to make the *Billboard* top 50 in America and only briefly scraped into the British charts at 39. As is often the way with legal disputes, in the end it had done neither party any good.

THE WAYWARD WIND

The reasons for Geffen's misgivings about Young's country album become apparent on the opening track of *Old Ways*. This is not some *Harvest*-style, easy-listening soft-rock album but hardcore cowboy music. "The Wayward Wind" was not even a Young composition but a cover of a song that had already been a hit for Tex Ritter and the Australian balladeer Frank Ifield. Waylon Jennings, the original Nashville "outlaw" plays guitar and Denise Draper becomes the latest in the line of female vocal accompanists that had included Emmylou Harris, Linda Ronstadt and Nicolette Larson.

WAYLON JENNINGS, ONE OF THE ARISTOCRATS OF COUNTRY MUSIC.

GET BACK TO THE COUNTRY

Fiddle and twanging jew's harp introduce "Get Back To The Country" and suddenly you realize that Young is genuinely committed both to the idiom and the good ol' boy philosophy behind it. The song is almost a hillbilly rewrite of the epic "Don't Be Denied" from *Times Fades Away* with a lyric in which he claims that even during the rock'n'roll years he always knew he would "get back to where it all began... back in the barn again."

He readily expanded on such downhome sentiments in interviews. Claiming that rock'n'roll "doesn't leave you a way to grow old gracefully and continue to work" he cited approvingly the example of 75-year-old country musicians who were still on the road doing what they had always done. He was "bored" with rock and "rowdy" guitar solos and declared that country music was far more amenable to someone of his age. "I guess I finally found something that I can believe in. I feel really good about the sincerity of the music."

ARE THERE ANY MORE REAL COWBOYS?

It was during the making of a video to accompany "Are There Any More Real Cowboys?" that Willie Nelson first suggested a benefit concert to help American farmers, along the lines of the Live Aid concert to relieve famine in the Horn of Africa. The conversation gave birth to Farm Aid, which was to become an annual event and which Young has supported tirelessly ever since. "If the administration continues on its present course, the family farmer in this country is finished," Young proselytized on the TV show *Good Morning America*.

The song expresses similar sentiments, as Young hopes the threatened lifestyle of the cattle rangers and "working cowboys" can be saved. Nelson then contributes a verse attacking the fake cowboys "who snort cocaine when the honky tonks all close" before Young shifts the focus back to "country families… trying hard to stay together and make a stand." The song encapsulates not only his romantic image of the lifestyle of the old West but also his increasingly right-wing views and the place of "family values" at the core of American patriotism. It was a stance that had led him to support many of the more reactionary policies of President Ronald Reagan, which, at one time, would have been anathema to him.

"A guy works for the living thing. He takes care of his family. Lives from day to day. It's the core of our whole country," he told *Rockbill*. "Working, taking care of your family, making life good, trying to be sincere about what you're doing. That's what America is supposed to be all about." Reagan himself never sounded more platitudinous. When Stephen Stills heard what he called such "ill-considered remarks" he refused to believe Young was serious.

"WHENEVER I TRY TO DO SOMETHING DIFFERENT EVERYBODY TELLS ME NOT TO DO IT."
NEIL YOUNG

ONCE AN ANGEL

Family values are again prominent in "Once An Angel", a sentimental ballad which celebrates "six years since my ring slipped on your finger". The arithmetic suggests the song is autobiographical and Young is singing about his own wife Pegi. In the second verse he confesses to treating her "so badly" but in true "Stand By Your Man" fashion, Young's "angel" hides her tears and takes him back.

Did his guilt relate to some real-life ill-treatment of his wife or was Young merely playing with the stereotypical plot lines of a country weepie? Unfortunately, he doesn't tell. But despite Stills' incredulity that Young could have grown so conservative, there's little doubt that his belief in the sanctity of the family as the rock on which the American way of life is founded was genuine. "A man gets up in the morning, goes to work, comes back, kisses his wife, they put food on the table, kids go to bed, watch TV for a while, maybe make love and go to sleep. That's not newsworthy, but that's what's happening. That's peacefulness," he said in a simplistic eulogy to the kind of ordinary family life that he himself would surely have found stupefyingly boring inside a week.

MISFITS

With " Misfits", Young almost forgot his determination not to deliver "the mother lode" to Geffen and few will argue with Johnny Rogan's judgement that it is his best song from the five albums he made for the label between 1983 and 1987.

As with many of Young's better songs, it's the product of what he called "automatic writing", composed spontaneously in the studio, and its surreal narrative recalls such epics as "Broken Arrow" and "Last Trip To Tulsa". "Misfits" starts on a space station with a crew of astronauts watching old Cassius Clay fights before the scene shifts to a hooker on a Texas sidewalk and a rodeo rider who drinks whisky all day. "There are a lot of science fiction overtones, time travel overtones in 'Misfits'. People at different places, geographically," he told *Melody Maker*'s Adam Sweeting. "All of the scenes in that song could have been happening simultaneously and yet they're also separate."

Country legend Waylon Jennings, who sings on the track, described the recording session as "the most fun I've had in 100 years." Impressed with Young's spontaneity, Jennings described the process. "There's a funny thing about his songs. He would come in with something and start singing it. Now I'm a songwriter, too, and I reckon I can judge a tune. I'd listen and I'd be thinking, 'That ain't gonna make it, hoss! That's not good'. But then in the studio he'd get a groove with it and it would turn out wonderful, just because it was so different. Sometimes I'd turn out to be right after all. But 80 per cent of the time he managed to prove me wrong."

CALIFORNIA SUNSET

Austin, Texas, is one of the most musical cities in the United States and the "anti-Nashville" alternative capital of country. A liberal, bohemian oasis in the redneck Lone Star State, it has, since the 1960s, been a magnet for musicians and a centre for country musicians who felt unhappy with the sterile, formulaic approach of Nashville. The most prominent Austinites included Willie Nelson and Jerry Jeff Walker.

Young visited Austin during 1984 on tour with the International Harvesters. At the time he was eschewing rock venues and playing venues such as Gilley's Rodeo Arena in Pasadena and even the Grand Ole Opry itself in Nashville. In September 1984, he played Austin City Limits, the PBS TV concert that had been showcasing the city's vibrant music scene since 1976 and continues as an institution to this day.

"California Sunset" was recorded during the performance and is notable for impressive contributions from Spooner Oldham on piano and Louisiana fiddler Rufus Thibodeaux. Young clearly enjoyed the Austin vibe and returned the following year on July 4, 1985, to appear at Willie Nelson's annual Independence Day "picnic", an event promoted as a "country Woodstock" and where he sang duets not only with Nelson but with Waylon Jennings and Jerry Jeff Walker.

Austin retains its "alternative" reputation to this day and every March hosts South By South West, a week-long showcase of up to 500 bands playing all over town, which has earned the description of the "coolest music festival in the world".

OLD WAYS

You'd have thought that Young's "rust never sleeps" philosophy would have meant that he found "old ways" anathema. On the release of his country album, however, he told the *Gainesville Sun*: "Growing old and trying to preserve tradition, all these things and family life, they're very important to me now."

The album's title song is playful and deliberately ambiguous. "It's hard to teach a dinosaur a new trick," he sings. Although he admits "old ways" can be "a ball and chain" he finds a certain comfort in their familiarity. The song also finds Young pledging to "stop that grass and give up all this

FROM ELECTRO TO C&W IN ONE GIANT STEP – THE CONTRADICTORY NEIL YOUNG.

drinking" and "clean up my whole way of living". But he goes to a party and the "old ways" win again.

After the album's release Young announced he was going on a diet of water and fruit juice to purge his body, a regime which appears to have lasted about as long in real life as it does in the song.

MY BOY

While devoting so much time to his second son Ben, Young had been stung by allegations that he had been neglecting his first son, Zeke, who was almost 14 by the time *Old Ways* was released. "Why you growing up so fast, my son?" he sings tenderly to his first born on "My Boy". The song risks descending into mawkishness but is saved by the obvious sincerity of Young's vocal. The song was written around the same time as a hearing in the LA Superior Court in which Zeke's mother, Carrie Snodgrass, had contested the informal financial settlement Young had made to take care of his son. Zeke later worked with his father as part of his road crew.

BOUND FOR GLORY

The voice of Waylon Jennings is again prominent on "Bound For Glory". Young had toured with Jennings and his wife Jessi Colter in 1984 and had been greatly influenced by the country singer, who was almost a decade older and had written the classic "Are You Sure Hank Done It This Way?" Jennings, in turn, was impressed with Young's love of country music. "He was a real country fan, pure and simple," he said. "We went out and did shows together for a while. You don't do that unless you mean it. He didn't have to do that."

Jennings was one of the leaders of country's "Outlaw" movement, so called for its refusal to follow the formulaic, production-line style of the Nashville studios to recording. Politically, however, he was innately conservative, which many felt helped to influence Young's increasingly hawkish views. "I stand by Reagan when it comes to (arms) build-up, to stand, to be able to play hardball with other countries that are aggressive towards free countries," Young told *Melody Maker*'s Adam Sweeting in 1985. At the start of the 1980s and the *Hawks And Doves* album, there had been some ambiguity about which side Young was on. By the middle of the decade there was no doubt.

The song itself is a typical Nashville story of marital infidelity. "I wrote that one on a word processor in the back of my bus," he told Bill Flanagan. "I wrote it with a couple of beers and a little smoke. The bus was rolling down the road and I typed it out. I knew the melody in my head already." This is hardly surprising. The tune bears such a close similarity to John Hartford's "Gentle On My Mind" that it's a wonder the writer didn't sue for royalties.

NEIL YOUNG'S UNPREDICTABILITY MADE THE 1980S A DIFFICULT DECADE FOR DIE-HARD FANS.

WHERE IS THE HIGHWAY TONIGHT

Around the same time as *Old Ways* was being released, two other developments were taking place in country music. One was the emergence in Nashville of a group of acts known as "new country" led by Steve Earle and Lyle Lovett among others, who sought to push the envelope and release country music from its clichés. The other was the movement in LA known as "cow punk", led by groups such as Lone Justice and Blood On The Saddle, which similarly took country music and injected it with an alternative rock sensibility.

Young, who from new wave to grunge has prided himself throughout his career on being at the cutting edge, had no association with either movement. On songs such as "Where Is The Highway Tonight?" he instead harked back to an older mainstream style of country developed by Chet Atkins and the other Nashville studio producers of the 1950s and 1960s. The truth was that *Old Ways* was every bit as retro and conservative an album as its 1950s-styled predecessor *Everybody's Rockin'*.

LANDING ON WATER

Recorded	August 1983 to March 1986, Los Angeles and Woodside, California.
Produced by	Danny Kortchmar, Neil Young.
Musicians	Neil Young (vocals, lead guitar, synthesizer), Steve Jordan (drums, synthesizer, vocals), Danny Kortchmar (guitar, synthesizer, vocals), San Francisco Boys Chorus (vocals)

WEIGHT OF THE WORLD
VIOLENT SIDE
HIPPIE DREAM
BAD NEWS BEAT
TOUCH THE NIGHT
PEOPLE ON THE STREET
HARD LUCK STORIES
I GOT A PROBLEM
PRESSURE
DRIFTER

"Rock'n'roll to me, I look at it and it looks like a dead-end street," Neil Young claimed in 1985. The follow-up to *Old Ways*, he insisted, would be another country album. "But it'll be a little bit harder. I'll play a little more electric guitar on it. I'm bringing rock'n'roll and country a little more together." The description might easily have fitted *Guitar Town*, the ground-breaking "new country" album that Steve Earle was about to issue on MCA. But it certainly didn't describe *Landing On Water*, Young's next release, which appeared in July 1986.

In pursuit of his country follow-up, Young had returned to Nashville after *Old Ways* to record a dozen further songs. Instead, however, he finally decided to give David Geffen the contemporary electric rock album he had been wanting since he had signed Young four years earlier. "One morning I woke up and all I could hear was this massive fucking beat. And my guitar was just rising out of it. I just heard rock'n'roll in my head so fucking loud that I couldn't ignore it," Young told *Rolling Stone* when asked to explain his volte-face. "Something came alive. It was like a bear waking up."

"IT'S A PIECE OF CRAP!" YOUNG'S RETROSPECTIVE VIEW OF *LANDING ON WATER*

However, *Landing On Water* merely exacerbated Geffen's frustration with his big signing. It was not the return to the raw and earthy sound of Crazy Horse that had driven Young's classic rock albums. Instead of Crazy Horse, he recruited on bass Danny Kortchmar, a noted guitarist who was responsible for the eloquent solo on Carole King's classic hit "It's Too Late", and session drummer Steve Jordan.

Despite the fact that Young had told the *Gainesville Sun* only months before that he would never make "a trendy, synthesizer based rock'n'roll record" because he was "bored" by the idea, with typical perversity that's precisely what he went and did. The results were dense, unrelenting and somewhat remorseless.

In self-defence, Young pointed out that the sessions for the album had been cut short by Geffen when he had exceeded his recording budget. Yet he was fully aware of the album's short-comings. "I was feeling tentative about the record and how people would like it," he said. The album's title had come to him on a flight when he been looking at the safety instructions covering an emergency landing on water. "I looked down at those people in the diagram and the big plane with the water lapping up the window. They were trying to get their rafts out of the doors and following directions. It didn't look like they had a chance. I kind of felt like that myself."

A year later he was even more honest about the album. "It's a piece of crap," he freely admitted. *Landing On Water* left Young's critical and commercial stock at an all-time low. Fortunately, there was only more album to go before his commitment to Geffen Records was up and something approaching normal service could be resumed on his return to Reprise.

WEIGHT OF THE WORLD

Clearly, Young had not worked his fascination with synths and electronica out of his system with *Trans*. "Weight Of The World" could almost have come from that album except that the vocoder has thankfully been mothballed. The riff goes nowhere and the lyric in which Young paints a picture of himself as a care-worn loner is mundane. Even on albums such as *Trans*, Young had been challenging and annoying. Here he commits the cardinal sun of sounding merely dull.

YOUNG'S DEAL WITH GEFFEN HAD BEEN A DISASTER FROM DAY ONE. NOW THE NIGHTMARE WAS ALMOST OVER.

VIOLENT SIDE

Anger management is the theme of "Violent Side", another song characterized by relentless synth drums. "Control the violent side," Young sings repeatedly with accompaniment from the San Francisco Boys' Chorus. It could have been an interesting idea for a song and the choir adds a different element but it's an opportunity wasted.

HIPPIE DREAM

By the time *Lands On Water* was released in the summer of 1986 David Crosby was in a bad way. The hippie dreams of the late 1960s and early 1970s, and the Woodstock spirit of peace, love and music, had given way a hell of paranoia, guns and free-base cocaine.

Crosby had epitomized the era. But by 1983, years of abuse had seen him lose all his earnings from the Byrds and CSNY on drugs and he had been sentenced to five years in jail in a Dallas courtroom for possession of cocaine and a firearm. Young could barely conceal his disgust at the bloated, impossible character Crosby had become. Then, while his sentence was under appeal, Crosby decided the best way to stay out of jail was to go on the run. He eventually surrendered in December 1985 and Young made him a promise.

"Everybody's concerned about David," he told a syndicated radio talk show at the time. "He's a unique person and has a lot of problems that are unique to him. He's having a rough time. He really took a bad turn. I hope he gets himself together. I've told him that if he does get himself together and straightens up that I'll join the group again and we'll do something together."

"Hippie Dream," the best song on *Landing On Water*, is directly addressed to Crosby, taking as its starting pointing his classic song *Wooden Ships* on the first CSN album. "The wooden ships were just a hippie dream," Young sings before he gets even more personal. "Another flower child gone to seed in an ether-filled room of meat hooks, it's so ugly." The ether was a reference to the virtual chemistry laboratory that Crosby carried with him at all times to prepare his drugs.

On his parole from jail in August 1986, a rehabilitated Crosby magnanimously forgave Young for the song. "I understand why he did it," he told Johnny Rogan. "You see, Neil loves me, man, and that was frustration. He and I are really good friends. He's one of the people who tried to help me get off drugs... he felt let down. That's why he wrote the song."

Young clearly felt a little guilty. By October he was fudging the focus of the song and claiming, "A lot of people think it was just about David Crosby, but really the whole thing is about me and about all kinds of different things." They included, he said, "What's happening to rock'n'roll? Where is the spirit?"

Young went on to keep his promise to Crosby, recording the 1989 album *American Dream* with CSNY, the first studio release by the foursome since 1970.

BAD NEWS BEAT

"Bad News Beat" may be the album's worst song, although there is strong competition from at least two other tracks. The melody is unmemorable and the lyric – about losing a girlfriend to a rival – collapses under the extended "bad news" metaphor with references to "bulletin" of blues and "late-breaking" disasters.

TOUCH THE NIGHT

NEIL YOUNG AND DAVID CROSBY – A LONG-STANDING FRIENDSHIP THAT HAS ENDURED MANY TWISTS AND TURNS.

An intriguing lyric of some promise about a road accident in which the driver walks away "without a scratch" is left undeveloped and thus "Touch The Night" sinks beneath a quagmire of unimaginative hard rock riffing. The lack of imagination is evidenced by the fact the melody is half borrowed from "Words (Between The Lines Of Age)", which had appeared on *Harvest*.

PEOPLE ON THE STREET

Another banal number with a tiresomely repetitive synth part as Young repeatedly tells us that "people on the street need a place to go".

HARD LUCK STORIES

Depressingly, *Landing On Water* just keeps on getting worse. "Hard Luck Stories" is more of the same, with a monotonous beat, a minimal tune and a lyric notable for its lack of compassion as Young tells an old friend to stop calling with his tales of bad luck and go get a life. The song could be another reference to Crosby and his problems, but there's no documented evidence to suggest that it is.

I GOT A PROBLEM

Another song of little merit with a heavy metal guitar riff and a echo-laden 1950s-sounding vocal that recalls the fiasco that was *Everybody's Rockin'*. "There must be some way out of here," Young sings in a line that repeats the opening words of Dylan's "All Along The Watchtower". He never gets around to telling us what the problem is but there's nothing much in the song to make you really care.

PRESSURE

A cry against the rat race and perhaps against the business pressures Young had experienced since signing for Geffen, "Pressure" is again ruined by a dull melody and rendered risible by its Devo-like chorus. The one point of interest is that the song betrays his contempt for the recently arrived MTV, which had started in 1981 and three years later was making an annual profit of six million dollars.

DRIFTER

That the indifferent "Drifter" is one of *Land On Water*'s highlights speaks volumes about an album that Young himself considered among his weakest. With lines such as "don't try to fence me in, don't try to slow me down" the song repeats his familiar "rust never sleeps" philosophy. But the song is left still-born by the arrangement, even if Young's voice and guitar work lifts the track above most of the rest of the album.

LIFE

Recorded: November 1986, Universal City, Los Angeles, California.

Produced by: Neil Young, David Briggs, Jack Nitzsche.

Musicians: Neil Young and Crazy Horse: Neil Young (vocals, guitar, harmonica, keyboards), Frank Sampedro (guitar, keyboards), Ralph Molina (drums), Billy Talbot (bass).

MIDEAST VACATION
LONG WALK HOME
AROUND THE WORLD
INCA QUEEN
TOO LONELY
PRISONERS OF ROCK'N'ROLL
CRYIN' EYES
WHEN YOUR LONELY HEART BREAKS
WE NEVER DANCED

The first Springfield reunion in almost 20 years occurred when all five original members assembled at Stephen Stills' house in Bel Air in July 1986 just as the woeful *Landing On Water* was being released. They reminisced, jammed and even discussed a reunion concert, although all the talk eventually came to nothing.

True to the promise Young had made to David Crosby, the CSNY reunion took place in the fall of 1986 at the first Bridge School Benefit concert in aid of a charity for handicapped children, founded by Young and his wife Pegi. It led to two full CSNY tours the following year and the *American Dream* album, which was released in 1989.

"I'M TIRED OF LISTENING TO PEOPLE SAY THAT AMERICA IS BAD EVERYWHERE... THAT OUR INVOLVEMENT IN CENTRAL AMERICA IS WRONG... THAT WE'RE A BUNCH OF AGGRESSIVE ANIMALS."
YOUNG'S POLITICS ALIENATED SOME OF HIS FANBASE

Then there were his most enduring and patient musical partners in Crazy Horse. Young's last album with them had been 1983's *Trans* and they had not been entirely comfortable with its electronic synth rock. But they were ready and waiting when he called to propose a 40-date American tour across the latter part of 1986 and the beginning of 1987.

Billing themselves as "the third best garage band in the world", it wasn't a happy tour and there was some ugly friction with bass player Billy Talbot, who was at the time drinking heavily and struggling to keep up. Nevertheless, they also made it to Europe and in between recorded *Life*, an album that was welcomed by those fans Young hadn't driven away for good as a welcome return to form. Not that it did his commercial standing too much good, peaking at No. 71 in Britain and at No. 75 in America.

In retrospect, it's a patchy album that doesn't rise to the standard of even his weakest 1970s work. But there are several impressive songs, mercifully the synths are not allowed to dominate and Young's voice is in great shape. "The whole thing about *Life* is that it was a sentence. A prison sentence. *Life*. That's how I meant it," he told *Select* in 1990.

Although one of the songs on *Life* was called "Prisoners Of Rock'n'Roll" and Young undoubtedly saw Geffen as his jailer, it's an odd comment under the circumstances. *Life* was his last album for the label. His sentence was not for life but had lasted five years and five albums. Furthermore, he was about to be "released".

Another interpretation lies in a subtle variant on the meaning of the word "lifer" put forward by Peter Buck. "There are those who go into rock'n'roll as a career option knowing that if it doesn't work they can become a banker or go to law school," the R.E.M. guitarist told me in 2001. "And then there are those I call 'the lifers' who do it because they can't do anything else and wouldn't be happy doing anything else." Under Buck's definition, Young has always been a lifer.

SOME FELT THAT NEIL YOUNG'S APPARENT RIGHT-WING POLITICS WERE AT ODDS WITH HIS "ROMANTIC TROUBADOUR" OF THE 1970S.

MIDEAST VACATION

Young's transformation into a flag-waving, Reagan-supporting American patriot had attracted a lot of criticism. "Reagan? So what if he is a trigger-happy cowboy?" he even said at one point in 1984 when the threat of the world destroying itself in a nuclear holocaust appeared to be at its height. "It makes me mad when people have that attitude, like from the 1960s – very idealistic, don't hurt anybody. I'm tired of listening to people say that America is bad everywhere, that our involvement in Central America is wrong, that we're a bunch of aggressive animals and don't have any cool."

In other interviews, he supported the US nuclear arms build-up against the Soviet Union, insisting "it was wrong to have let the armed forces deteriorate". He even went so far as to suggest that America had only been "trying to help" in Vietnam.

"Mideast Vacation" finds the song's protagonist stuck in a demonstration and surrounded by protesters chanting "death to America". In fact, Young may even be describing Reagan himself because the character travels to meet the Libyan leader Colonel Gadaffi on *Air Force One*, the presidential plane. Maddened by the taunts, the figure turns into "Rambo in a disco", an all-American action man fighting for his country's honour. The mob responds by burning his effigy, a familiar middle-eastern response to the American president at the time.

The song has since divided the critics. Rogan is generous in his admiration for Young's "black humour". But if it was a joke, Allan Jones in *Melody Maker* certainly didn't find it funny and denounced the song as a piece of "ill-tempered patriotic posturing." Sylvie Simmons in her brief 2001 biography in the *Mojo Heroes* series is even more damning. In the roll-call of rock'n'roll shame, she goes as far as ranking Young's pro-Reagan speeches alongside the infamous Nazi salute David Bowie gave in the mid-1970s.

LONG WALK HOME

"Long Walk Home" finds Young offering further observations on "liberty" and America's "the search for truth" from "Vietnam to old Beirut". There's a hint that international politics is more than a fight between the goodies and the baddies in the line "why do we feel the double-edged blade cutting through our hands?" But many found Young's righteous belief in America's role as the guardian of the world's freedom hard to stomach. The song's gentle, yearning style appears out of step with the sentiments, particularly when the reverie is interrupted by bursts of mock gunfire.

Most astonishing of all, before the album's release, both "Mideast Vacation" and "Long Walk Home" were played by CSNY in concert in Santa Barbara in February 1987. Given the group's long-standing commitment to radical causes, the notion of Crosby, Stills and Nash harmonizing on Young's paeans to Reaganism was positively surreal.

AROUND THE WORLD

With the third successive song with a political theme, *Life* begins to resemble a concept album, although fortunately one that peters out after "Around The World". Politically it's the least gung-ho and xenophobic of the trilogy, as Young wryly observes that world leaders change as regularly as "fashions" and "style," although the suggestion is still that the American way will always prevail.

"I wrote it in Daytona Beach when I was real sick with flu," Young later explained and there's a distinctly feverish quality to its unrelenting beat.

INCA QUEEN

Young had first visited South American history on "Cortez The Killer" in 1975, when he had considered an entire album around the themes of time travel and ancient civilizations. Whether "Inca Queen" was originally written for that project is unclear. Certainly both themes are present as Young's Inca monarch is visited by "silver (spaceships) from the skies". The theory that the world's most ancient civilizations were in contact with extra-terrestrial beings had been given considerable currency by books such as Erich Von Daniken's *Chariots Of The Gods*, and Young was clearly fascinated by the theme, having first alluded to it on "After The Gold Rush".

TOO LONELY

Back in 1967, Young had blatantly plagiarized the Rolling Stones' "(I Can't Get No) Satisfaction)" to dramatic effect on Buffalo Springfield's "Mr Soul". On "Too Lonely" he visits the Jagger-Richards tune again.

PRISONERS OF ROCK'N'ROLL

Young knew *Life* was his last album for Geffen and, given the history of the relationship and the attempt to sue him, perhaps he would have been less than human if he hadn't taken the opportunity to chide the record company that had caused him so much grief. "We never listen to the record company man, he tried to change us and ruin our band," Young sings on "Prisoners of Rock'n'Roll" over a simplistic tune, but with more passion than he'd mustered in a long time.

CRYIN' EYES

When the chemistry between Young and Crazy Horse was at its best they were capable of producing some of the most visceral music in rock'n'roll. "Cryin' Eyes" finds them almost back to their storming best on a song that Young had first unveiled with the Ducks on their Californian bars tour in 1977. Some hardcore fans who have heard bootlegged tapes of those shows claim that the Ducks' version from a decade earlier was superior.

WHEN YOUR LONELY HEART BREAKS

That Young could still write great love songs in the classic singer-songwriter style of *Harvest* is proved by "When Your Lonely Heart Breaks". His voice is high, lonesome and aching and the melody is lovely. Unfortunately the track is let down by a dated 1980s-style production.

WE NEVER DANCED

While recording "We Never Danced" in early 1987, Young must have felt that he'd travelled back in time 20 years to the days when he had first quit Buffalo Springfield and had begun working with Jack Nitzsche.

After the informal Springfield reunion at Stills's house in July 1986, Young had agreed to a further session – and promptly forgotten all about it. When the other four original Springfield members assembled as agreed, there was no sign of Young. According to Bruce Palmer, they waited two hours and eventually tracked him down to Sunset Sound, Hollywood, where he was in the studio. "His excuse was that he forgot," Palmer later recalled. Young apologized, but when asked to drop what he was doing and come over as agreed he insisted, "I can't. I've got 16 musicians in the studio. I've got Jack Nitzsche. I can't do it now." Palmer could not hide his anger: "I immediately realized that I was still dealing with the same self-righteous, cold-hearted son of a bitch, that doesn't give a damn about anybody other than himself," he fumed.

The track Young was recording was "We Never Danced", a song written for the movie *Made In Heaven* – hence the lyric about being reunited after death with a loved one. The melody recalled earlier Nitzsche-Young collaborations such as "Expecting To Fly". But he might have been better off attending the Springfield reunion because Young's version of the song was rejected by the movie studio and Martha Davis, who had just left The Motels, was asked to sing it instead.

THIS NOTE'S FOR YOU

Recorded	November 1987 to January 1988, Hollywood, California.
Produced by	Neil Young, Niko Bolas.
Musicians	Neil Young (vocals, guitar), Chad Cromwell (drums), Rick Rosas (bass), Frank Sampedro (keyboards), Steve Lawrence (tenor saxophone), Ben Keith (alto saxophone), Larry Cragg (baritone saxophone), Claude Cailliet (trombone), John Fumo (trumpet), Tom Bray (trumpet).

TEN MEN WORKIN'
THIS NOTE'S FOR YOU
COUPE DE VILLE
LIFE IN THE CITY
TWILIGHT
MARRIED MAN
SUNNY INSIDE
CAN'T BELIEVE YOU'RE LYING
HEY HEY
ONE THING

THIS NOTE'S FOR YOU ALMOST REPRESENTED A RETURN TO FORM AFTER THE DISASTER OF YOUNG'S GEFFEN YEARS.

It was a mark of the esteem in which Young had been held in the 1970s that even after a series of seven disappointing – and sometimes execrable – albums, a frisson of excitement greeted the announcement of his first recording back on Warner/Reprise after the disastrous Geffen years.

Despite the vocoder, the 24-minute rockabilly rip-off, the redneck album, the horrible synth-rock and even the obscene spectacle of his political love-in with Ronald Reagan, his fans never *quite* surrendered all hope. *This Note's For You* might not make it into a list of Young's all-time top five albums. But in the light of what had gone before, it felt like manna from heaven after a plague of frogs, locusts and worse.

As with so many of Young's projects, *This Note's For You* had a somewhat tortuous gestation. After a trip to Canada in 1986 when he was reunited with members of his first band the Squires, whose repertoire had been strongly blues-influenced, Young found himself composing a bunch of new songs in similar vein. Taking to the road with Crazy Horse, he began playing the blues-flavoured songs and soon his imagination was running riot.

At first, he envisaged a film about a bunch of middle-aged blues musicians who had never cracked it commercially but still get off on what they do. The imaginary movie swiftly turned into a search for just such a real-life band. "I thought if I'm really going to do this, I'll have to get a band for real, get some characters and some horns and make it really swing," Young said.

He had hoped that Crazy Horse, augmented by a horn section, could be that band and he proposed renaming them The Blue Notes for the project. But, not for the first time, after some low-key live performances around San Francisco, he decided that the Crazy Horse rhythm section of Talbot and Molina weren't up to the job. In their place he recruited drummer Chad Cromwell and bassist Rick Rosas and, to add insult to injury, decided to retain Crazy Horse guitarist Frank Sampedro as a keyboard player.

An album of ten songs was completed in record time and Young dubbed the sound "the dawn of power swing". He also invited Frank Sinatra – the man who had founded the Reprise label in 1960 with specific instructions *never* to release any rock and roll music – to guest on the album. The invitation was declined.

Young approached *This Note's For You* with gusto. "I'm creating a life's work and the Blue Notes feel really right to me. It's easier for me to sing this music than any other music I've ever sung. It may be I should have been doing this all my life," he enthused to the San Francisco music paper *BAM*. "I've played all kinds of music all the time since the very beginning. The changes in style have just become more radical in the last decade that's all."

TEN MEN WORKIN'

The 1970s soul singer Harold Melvin – whose famous backing group were also called the Blue Notes – had sued over the name when Young started using it on tour in 1987 before the album's release. Young responded promptly by changing the band's name to "Ten Men Workin'", and the song that bears the same title, with its punching six-strong brass section, can be viewed as a manifesto of his new musical mission – "We are men at work, we got a job to do, we gotta keep you rockin', to keep your soul from the blue."

He had taken the name from a "Men At Work" t-shirt, sported by an engineer who was working on his boat. "I just kept looking at that t-shirt and started thinking. 'Yeah, that's me. I'm working and we're working'. It's like we were building or something. We had this job to do. It was like it was our mission to make people feel good and to make them dance," he told the San Francisco paper BAM.

In its way, *This Note's For You* is as much a genre album as any of Young's other 1980s recordings. Yet it succeeds where the likes of *Trans* and *Everybody's Rockin'* failed. Where those records too often sounded like pastiche, here there's a clear commitment and belief that lends the entire album a unifying coherence.

THIS NOTE'S FOR YOU

By the late 1980s the once rebellious spirit of rock'n'roll had been corporatized. No big rock tour was complete without a commercial sponsor and Young hated the idea of stages festooned with company logos. At the same time, rock stars such as Michael Jackson were being paid huge amounts of money by companies such as Pepsi to endorse their products in TV commercials.

Young was having none of it. "Ain't singing for Pepsi, ain't singing for Coke, makes me look like a joke," he sings in an open reference to Jackson's "sell-out". The beer companies Miller and Budweiser are similarly dismissed and indeed the entire song is a take-off of the beer ad jingle "This Bud's For You". Yet Young also can't resist a poke at his old benefit-playing colleagues in CSN when he adds that he won't sing for politicians, either.

MICHAEL JACKSON – UNLIKE NEIL YOUNG, HE *DID* SING FOR PEPSI.

The video that accompanied the single was directed by Julien Temple, who had been responsible for the Sex Pistols' movie *The Great Rock'n'Roll Swindle*. Containing scenes that satirized TV adverts for all of the products named in the song as well as parodies of Jackson, Eric Clapton and Whitney Houston, MTV banned the video on the grounds that it infringed rules on product placement. Later the station reversed the decision and – with supreme irony – the film went on to win an MTV award as video of the year.

Not everyone was amused. A furious Glenn Frey of the Eagles, who had just signed a one million dollar contract with

Pepsi, accused Young of "setting himself up as rock'n'roll's conscience" and branded him a hypocrite.

Young admitted there were inconsistencies in his position. But he stuck to his anti-corporate guns. "I have to play the Budweiser concert series because they made a deal with the promoter," he told Johnny Rogan. "I can't get around it but I want people to know that it's not me making the deal with Budweiser and Miller. They bought all the places where I play."

He was also surprised by the song's success. "I remember writing it on my bus and turning to my driver and saying, 'Jesus Christ, this must be the most idiotic fucking song I've ever written.' I still can't believe that such a dumb little song could have helped resuscitate my career the way it did."

COUPE DE VILLE

The entire concept of *This Note's For You* romanticizes the notion of working musicians out on the road playing every night for the thrill of it. But Young knew as well as anyone that the touring life is a hard one with its endless round of late nights, travelling, sound checks, late nights and more travelling.

In "Coup de Ville" he describes "hitting the wall" late one night in his hotel room after a gig. Young explained the song's creation to *Musician* magazine: "I'd been working really hard for a number of weeks and I was very tired. I hadn't been sleeping that well and I was up early and writing the song and breakfast came. I started eating and then I started feeling dizzy and really sick. Then I went back to bed and started to go to sleep. And then I realized that's it. I hit the wall, that's what it was. And I was right back up and finishing the song. It was over before I remembered that I had gotten dizzy and felt sick. So I went back to sleep. That's how things happen. There's no method."

LIFE IN THE CITY

After his patriotic support for Reagan's apple-pie fantasy of the all-American way of life, on "Life In The City" Young examines to the darker, seamier side of the dream. Portraying a scary vision of a city ravaged by crime in which starving people sleep on sidewalks, he notes acerbically, "It's the American way". He even laments the plight of "families in need" and his apparent compassion is a far cry from a misguided comment two years earlier, in which he had claimed, "Americans need to stop being supported by the government and get out to work. You can't always support the weak."

TWILIGHT

For a great songwriter, Young can sometimes descend into the most overused clichés and "Twilight" is a case in point. In the song time "stands still", his girlfriend is "the best thing I ever had", true love is "hard to find" and the sun sets "on the long road home".

Thanks to a hauntingly inventive arrangement and some moody guitar playing, he gets away with it and imbues "Twilight" with a heartfelt longing for Pegi and his family "waitin' by the front door" while he and his "men at work" are out on the road.

MARRIED MAN

The temptations of the touring life are well documented and in "Married Man" Young again reminds the ladies of the road of his marital status. The brass section swings exuberantly and the song has a spontaneous flow – indeed, it was written on the way to the studio and recorded instantly.

SUNNY INSIDE

Young had first attempted to record "Sunny Inside" with Crazy Horse for *Trans* but it did not fit that album's computer age theme. The song would undoubtedly have lifted the record, although it surely would not have sounded as good with synths and a vocoder as it does here with its joyous brass and Stax-style riff.

CAN'T BELIEVE YOU'RE LYING

The lyin' cheatin' woman who takes her lover for a ride and leaves him when she's spent all his money is a familiar theme of the blues song.

On "Can't Believe You're Lyin'" Young delivers his take on the template in some style. Like the rest of the album, the feel is spontaneous and the song was recorded on the second take.

HEY HEY

Young again mines the imagery of traditional blues music for "Hey Hey". Despite the lyrical clichés he once more manages to sound fresh and interesting, partly by adding a contemporary flavour with another well-aimed jibe at MTV. Musically, it's a cross between a Chicago blues and a Louis Jordan-style jump boogie.

ONE THING

Despite a different line-up with Crazy Horse's Ralph Molina recalled from exile on drums and George Whitsell once of the pre-Crazy Horse Rockets on bass, "One Thing" retains the consistent mood of *This Note's For You*. It's another slow and atmospheric blues with a matching lyric about a doomed relationship. But even the blues can have a silver lining – in this instance the revival of Young's flagging career and a bout of inspiration that resulted in his best album in almost a decade.

MEN AT WORK! YOUNG AND HIS NEW COHORTS ROCK OUT DURING THEIR 1987 TOUR.

FREEDOM

Recorded	July 1988 to July 10, 1989, Woodside, California; New York City, New York.
Produced by	Neil Young, Niko Bolas.
Musicians	Neil Young (vocals, guitar, piano), Chad Cromwell (drums), Rick Rosas (bass), Frank Sampedro (guitar, keyboards, mandolin, vocals), Ben Keith (alto saxophone, pedal steel guitar, keyboards), Linda Ronstadt (vocals), Tony Marsico (bass), Steve Lawrence (tenor saxophone), Larry Cragg (baritone saxophone), Claude Cailliet (trombone), John Fumo (trumpet), Tom Bray (trumpet).

ROCKIN' IN THE FREE WORLD
CRIME IN THE CITY (SIXTY TO ZERO PART ONE)
DON'T CRY
HANGIN' ON A LIMB
ELDORADO
THE WAYS OF LOVE
SOMEDAY
ON BROADWAY
WRECKING BALL
NO MORE
TOO FAR GONE

NEIL YOUNG: THE GUITAR-WIELDING REVOLUTIONARY WITH A CAREER NOW FIRMLY BACK ON TRACK.

If *This Note's For You* had seen Young rising from the ashes of his own artistic self-immolation, then *Freedom* found him flying towards the sun again. Young himself was singularly unimpressed with talk of his alleged "return to form" and such comments tended to make him angry or sullen in interviews. "All these reviewers writing stuff about my comeback," he ranted at Nick Kent. "Listen, I don't have to come back because I've never been gone. They write stuff like 'Oh this year Neil Young's OK again.' Fuck them. I don't need them to tell me if I'm OK or not. As far as I'm concerned I've always been OK."

"I never went away. I just did other things. I'm not like some 1960s band coming back to take advantage of some wave of bullshit nostalgia. I mean, I'm someone who's always tried systematically to destroy the very basis of my record-buying public. My whole career is based on systematic destruction for years and years. See, that's what keeps me alive. You destroy what you did before and you're free to carry on. So I've been busy destroying all these things."

Over the years, the sincerity of such remarks has been debated by fans and critics alike. As an explanation for the undoubtedly poor albums Young has made at times in his career, the excuse can appear all too glib and just a little too convenient. But whatever Young's true motivation, there is no doubt that Freedom was his best album of the 1980s and that he deliberately set out to end the decade on a creative high, just as he had done when he had signed-off the 1970s with *Rust Never Sleeps*.

As so often the case with Young, the release went through several incarnations before he settled on *Freedom*. His first plan had been a live double album with the Blue Notes, who had gone on tour in April 1988 to promote *This Note's For You* and again in August. Young had written a new batch of compositions for the tour, which included "Ordinary People", "Days That Used To Be", "Sixty To Zero", "Fool For Your Love", "Doghouse" and "Boxcar".

When that projected release was abandoned, he next went into the Hit Factory studio in New York and recorded nine songs for an album provisionally titled Times Square. Then the name was changed to *Eldorado* and the release scaled down to a five-track EP, which Young peculiarly decided to release only in Japan. "I didn't want to put *Eldorado* out in the States and all over the place in the regular arena of records. I felt like it needed to be presented in a way that showed I really cared about it," he told MTV.

Clearly the hostile reception that had greeted most of his recent output had hurt. "Rather than going through all that bullshit with all the critics and everybody writing about it and saying I'm off on this trip, I decided not to let them do that this time," he said. "I let this one be for the people who want to listen to it."

After the Japanese release, it was another six months before the rest of the world would get a new Neil Young record, when *Freedom* was released in October 1989. His most successful effort in a decade, the album took six of the songs recorded for Times Square and added six new songs. Three of the five tracks from *Eldorado* – "Don't Cry", a cover of The Drifters' "On Broadway" and "Eldorado" – were included. But two heavy rock numbers, "Cocaine Eyes" and "Heavy Love", were not, and to this day remain officially available only on the Japanese EP.

ROCKIN' IN THE FREE WORLD

THE ALBUM'S OPENER PROVIDED A CONVENIENT TV BACKDROP TO THE DEMOLITION OF THE BERLIN WALL.

As the 1980s came to a close, the post-World War Two international order was crumbling. In the Soviet Union, Mikhail Gorbachev had introduced the era of *perestroika* and *glasnost* in which state authoritarianism and anti-western posturing was relaxed. Soon the old Communist regimes were crumbling all over eastern Europe. Poland embraced democracy and Hungary, the Czech Republic, Bulgaria and Romania were ready to follow suit. The Berlin Wall was about to be torn down and Germany reunited. The cold war was, in effect, over – and the "free world" had won.

Many of these events were yet to happen when Young recorded "Rockin' In The Free World" but they were already in train and there is no doubt that the song tapped into the zeitgeist to capture a moment of world-shattering change. Indeed, TV news footage of the Berlin Wall coming down was often accompanied by the strains of the song. But Young's composition is far subtler than that. It is undeniably anthemic, yet there's no hint of triumphalism. Instead, Young turns his focus on the heavy price that can accompany democracy and paints a nightmarish picture of a "free world" populated by derelicts, burnt-out cases and junkie mothers.

As a father he was particularly concerned about drugs on the streets of America. "The lyrics are just a description of events going on every day in America. Sure I'm concerned for my children, particularly my eldest son and he's a Guns'n'Roses fan," he told Nick Kent in Vox. "He has to face drugs every day in the school yard that are way stronger than anything I got offered in most of my years as a professional musician."

"This is like the Bible," he went on to warn apocalyptically. The "free world" was exporting all kinds of dangerous tendencies to the former Soviet bloc countries along with democracy. "It's all completely out of control. The drugs are gonna be all over the streets of Europe. We've got a lot to deal with here," Young opined.

Freedom contains two versions of "Rockin' In The Free World", which bookend the album. The first acoustic take, which opens the record, was recorded live at Jones Beach, Long Island. The second electric version, with an additional verse, makes for a dynamic album closer.

CRIME IN THE CITY (SIXTY TO ZERO PART ONE)

In the early summer of 1988, Young had set sail on his boat *W.N.Ragland* for Hawaii. Alone at sea he wrote three songs in a single night – "Days That Used To Be" (which would appear two years later on *Ragged Glory*), "Ordinary People" (which has never been released) and "Sixty To Zero".

Johnny Rogan was so taken with the later song that he borrowed the title for his magisterial 700-page biography, although the version that appears on *Freedom* is truncated from the original 11 verses Young had played live with the Blue Notes to just five verses.

In the tradition of earlier epics such as "Broken Arrow" and "Last Trip To Tulsa", "Crime In The City (60 To Zero Part One)" as the abbreviated version was renamed, contains a surreal narrative that suggests the influence of Bob Dylan, who around the same time had stayed on Young's ranch at La Honda. The song's chord structure bears a passing resemblance to Dylan's "All Along The Watchtower" and the five verses Young allows us jump from a bank robbery to a cynical record producer and a corrupt city cop. Even more interesting is the fourth stanza in which Young pours out his feelings about his parents' divorce in 1959.

As a teenage boy he continued to live with his mother Rassy. He saw his father Scott only sporadically and the family break-up had a profound effect. In 1997, in conversation with Rogan, Scott Young recalled the moment when he announced he was leaving. "We talked about the bare bones of what was going to happen next. Then we walked down the street," he recalled. "Neil patted me on the back almost as if he felt sorry for me and that was that."

"THEY WRITE STUFF LIKE 'OH, THIS YEAR NEIL YOUNG'S OK AGAIN.' FUCK THEM! I DON'T NEED THEM TO TELL ME IF I'M OK. AS FAR AS I'M CONCERNED I'VE ALWAYS BEEN OK!"
THE ARTIST GETS TESTY WITH THE PRESS

In the song written three decades later, Young does not keep his emotions in such close check. "Sometimes I talk to Daddy on the telephone/ When he says that he loves me I know that he does/ But I wish I could see him, I wish I knew where he was," he sings, as if it the wounds were still fresh. The final verse includes the line "I keep getting younger, my life's been funny that way" which recalls Dylan's "I was so much older then, I'm younger than that now" from his 1964 song, "My Back Pages".

DON'T CRY

Young had already recorded a song called "Don't Cry No Tears" on 1975's *Zuma*. The feedback-drenched "Don't Cry" revisits the theme of attempting to end a relationship with the minimum or rancour and to move on. "That's me totally under the influence of Roy Orbison," Young revealed. "When I wrote it and recorded it I was thinking Roy Orbison meets thrash metal."

HANGIN' ON A LIMB

Although *Freedom* is hardly a concept album, it's surely no coincidence that the word "free" or "freedom" occurs on three of the first four songs. The lovely acoustic "Hangin' On A Limb" also has Linda Ronstadt returning on backing vocals for the first time in a decade.

ELDORADO

Several critics have likened "Eldorado" to a spaghetti western with its cast of gypsies, gamblers and women "all dressed in diamonds and sable". David Crosby had done something similar with "Cowboy Movie" from his first solo album in 1970 and had later revealed that the characters in the song were actually based on CSNY and various members of their entourage. If there is any similar allegory at work here, Young has disguised it well, although half way through the song the western setting changes to a more contemporary scene and a shady deal of indeterminate nature involving jet planes and briefcases full of either drugs or cash.

THE WAYS OF LOVE

One of two older songs on *Freedom*, the tender ballad "The Ways Of Love" dates back to the 1970s and had first been played live by Young back in 1978. With Ben Keith's pedal steel prominent and Linda Ronstadt again on backing vocals, it recalls the spirit of that year's *Comes A Time*. "I did a session of older songs, some of them 15 years old. Just songs I had around," he explained in an interview on BBC Radio 1. "I got two, 'The Ways Of Love' and 'Too Far Gone' that I thought were good. So I had a base. People could hear these songs from *Freedom* and relate them to whatever it is they liked about me 15 years ago. It reaches back like a root."

SOMEDAY

At first "Someday" suggests it might be another of Young's semi-historical narratives, with an opening verse about the World War Two German field marshall Erwin Rommel, who supported the 1944 plot against Hitler and then committed suicide.

However, the song soon dissolves into an observation on TV preachers and Alaskan pipe workers for reasons that are unclear. But "Someday" possesses one of Young's strongest melodies and, with the six-strong horn section restored from *This Note's For You*, it's the closest he ever got to sounding like Bruce Springsteen.

ON BROADWAY

Originally a worldwide hit single for Ben E. King and The Drifters in 1963, "On Broadway" was written by the hugely successful hit-making team of Jerry Leiber and Mike Stoller.

The song's original lyric was barbed with disillusionment and Young's own cover gives the song an even darker contemporary twist with snarling feedback guitar. Towards the end it takes on a positively harrowing tone as Young demands "give me that crack", evidently a reference to the dealing he observed taking place on the street outside the Hit Factory studio on Broadway where he was recording.

WRECKING BALL

Young is such an individual writer and performer that it is rare for another artist to record the definitive version of one of his songs. However, Emmylou Harris arguably achieved just that when she covered "Wrecking Ball" and made it the title track of her stunning 1995 comeback album.

This is not to say that there is anything wrong with Young's original version, which has a haunting southern gothic feel. The wrecking ball of the title is "a place where you can go to dance with someone other than your wife and it wrecks your life," Young remarked in a comment that only underlined the song's appealing mystery.

NO MORE

"MY WHOLE CAREER IS BASED ON SYSTEMATIC DESTRUCTION… THAT'S WHAT KEEPS ME ALIVE… YOU DESTROY WHAT YOU DID BEFORE AND YOU'RE FREE TO CARRY ON."

Young's drug use had, to some extent, been restrained by his epileptic condition. However, throughout much of his adult life he has smoked marijuana and for a time in the 1970s was known to have used cocaine regularly. He had already chronicled his use of different drugs on "Hitchhiker", a song written in the mid-1970s, but which he never recorded, and "No More" returns to that theme. "Not so long ago it had a hold on me," he sings without ever revealing which drug he is talking about.

Although only Frank Sampedro (or "Poncho Villa", as Young re-christened him for the sleeve credits of *Freedom*) appears on "No More", musically the song returns to the trademark guitar-driven sound Young forged with the Crazy Horse in the 1970s.

FAR GONE

Like "The Ways Of Love", Young also resurrected "Too Far Gone" from the 1970s. He had premiered the song live during a concert in London in 1976 and it had been scheduled for inclusion on *Chrome Dreams*, the album which was then aborted in favour of *American Stars'n'Bars*. Crazy Horse's Frank Sampedro adds some attractive mandolin to the gentle country-tinged re-recorded version that turned up on *Freedom*, alongside Ben Keith's pedal steel.

RAGGED GLORY

Recorded	April 1990, Woodside, California.
Produced by	Neil Young and David Briggs.
Musicians	Neil Young and Crazy Horse: Neil Young (vocals, guitar, harmonica, keyboards), Frank Sampedro (guitar, keyboards), Ralph Molina (drums), Billy Talbot (bass).

COUNTRY HOME
WHITE LINE
FUCKIN' UP
OVER AND OVER
LOVE TO BURN
FARMER JOHN
MANSION ON THE HILL
DAYS THAT USED TO BE
LOVE AND ONLY LOVE
MOTHER EARTH (NATURAL ANTHEM)

If a scorched-earth policy towards his own myth had motivated Young's commercial and critical decline throughout most of the 1980s, then the 1990s was to prove to be the decade not merely of his resurrection but of his near-deification. Young himself adopted the metaphor of a car to describe the trajectory of his career.

"When I came out I was a very cool car. Then I got a bit used and there were all these other newer models and pretty soon it was time to put me in the junkyard and use me for parts," he told *The Times*. "Then for a long time it seemed like I must be falling apart, although that didn't bother me because inside I felt good about what I was doing. And finally people started going 'hey look at that over there, that's a classic. And it's in pretty good shape.'"

To put the classic model back on the road he invited Crazy Horse on board again and the engine purred with pleasure as *Ragged Glory*, his first album of the new decade, found him exploring highways he hadn't really been down since the 1970s. In fact, the best thing about Ragged Glory was that it sounded as if the 1980s had never happened.

Young had fallen out badly with Crazy Horse on the *Rusted Out Garage Tour* in 1986–87 and at the time of the release of Life had claimed he would never work with them again. "That was a bad period for us," he confessed to Nick Kent several years later. "We weren't playing well then and overall the material wasn't up to much."

"THE ENVIRONMENT IS REALLY IMPORTANT TO ME… AT LEAST FOR ME TO DO MY PART… AS MUCH AS I CAN TO KEEP THE BALL ROLLING FOR THE PLANET."

However, as the 1990s began, Young was able to look back more dispassionately and he concluded that he was missing the chemistry that Crazy Horse at their best were capable of generating. In February, he summoned the group to his ranch and offered to bury the hatchet. Within days they were recording together in his barn. "All the other groups are transient compared to Crazy Horse," he told MTV. "Crazy Horse and I are rock'n'roll. It's pretty primitive stuff. Simple. Anybody can play it that knows how to play it a little bit, but we just go for the feel."

Ragged Glory was released in September 1990 and the title perfectly encapsulated the style of playing. The album received even more euphoric reviews than *Freedom*, although it's worth recording the note of caution struck by Johnny Rogan, the doyen of Young commentators. While admiring the "raw excitement" of the recording, Rogan complained that the songs lack the power of Young's best work with Crazy Horse, such as "Cowgirl In The Sand" or "Cortez The Killer". However, for most of us, it was enough merely that Young was making records in something close to his "classic" style once again.

COUNTRY HOME

Part of the reason that *Ragged Glory* sounded like a 1970s Neil Young album was that several of its compositions were drawn from the era. "Country Home," a paean to Young's life on his ranch, was originally known as "Spud Blues" and includes an entire verse about a potato patch. Yet if the lyric is less than profound, the guitar work-out is superb, stretching the song to seven minutes while never outstaying its welcome.

WHITE LINE

Once again Young dips back into his 1970s songbook for a composition that was originally intended for inclusion on *Homegrown*, his mythical "lost" album scrapped in 1975. The "white lines" in the song have a double meaning, signifying both the markings on the thousands of miles of roads travelled by working musicians and the cocaine that all too often keeps them going.

FUCKIN' UP

Simple and repetitive but effective, "Fuckin' Up" came with a message that instantly hit a chord with the grunge movement emerging at the time around bands such as Nirvana. Inevitably there was some controversy over the song's title and radio play was limited as a result. Yet Young was unrepentant. "Everyone should play the song. I think it's one of the best rock'n'roll songs of all the songs I've ever done and I think the performance of it is at least as good as anything I've ever done," he said. "Of course it makes me sad that a lot of people won't hear it just because it has the word 'fuckin'' in it."

Young was particularly pleased that the song gave him a new relevance to what had become known as "Generation X" or the "slackers", late teenagers and young twentysomethings who had adopted grunge as their music of choice. "There's nothing different in what they're doing right now than what we were doing in the 1960s, even the audiences look and feel the same," he said proudly. Soon he was being referred to as "the godfather of grunge", an association that was cemented on the *Mirror Ball* album recorded with Pearl Jam as his backing band.

YOUNG KICKED OFF A NEW DECADE WITH A RENEWED PASSION, AND AN ALBUM THAT HARKED BACK TO HIS 70S CLASSICS.

OVER AND OVER

"Over And Over" is built around a classic Crazy Horse riff, although it was one that the band had some difficulty grasping initially. "The first time we were learning it we could never get it together," Young recalled. On the last occasion this had happened in the 1980s, Young had accused the band of not concentrating and dismissed them as a bunch of drunks. This time he adopted a more constructive if unconventional approach and left a message on guitarist Frank Sampedro's telephone answering machine. "OK Frank, this is it. It's like one, two, three, doo, doo, do." Sampedro played his voice mail message over and over until he got it and the song was nailed.

LOVE TO BURN

At over ten minutes in length, "Love To Burn" is Crazy Horse at their elongated, improvisational best – it's almost as if there is an alchemical understanding between Young and the band. The taut, physical anger of much of Young's electric music is still present but there's a joy and exhilaration, too. Writing in the English music magazine *Mojo* some years later, Nick Kent enthused that the guitar jam on "Love To Burn" was "every bit as ecstatic and spiritual as one of John Coltrane's classic extrapolations".

Young was similarly excited by Crazy Horse's playing. "I'm just a part of Crazy Horse. It's never me and Crazy Horse, whatever it says on the album sleeves. It's Crazy Horse," he insisted. "When there's a guitar solo of mine on a Crazy Horse record, it's not a guitar solo. It's an instrumental. It just doesn't happen without them. You hear me play with other people, my whole psychedelic side just doesn't happen because nobody but Crazy Horse can really bring it out of me."

FARMER JOHN

Written by Don & Dewey, and later a 1964 hit for Chicano beat group The Premiers, "Farmer John" is not much more than a jam, recorded on the last day of the *Ragged Glory* sessions when Young and Crazy Horse

CRAZY HORSE: BACK IN THE SADDLE AGAIN.

had, in an idle moment, started swapping stories of the first songs they had learned in high school bands.

The band were so carried away by the raucous version of "Farmer John" that ensued, that apparently nobody in the studio even noticed the minor earthquake that struck San Francisco while they were making the recording.

MANSION ON THE HILL

"I'M JUST A PART OF CRAZY HORSE. IT'S NEVER ME AND CRAZY HORSE... WHATEVER IT SAYS ON THE ALBUM."

Although Neil Young laid great store by his "rust theory" – moving forward and never standing still – the reality is that he is also fascinated to the point of obsession with his own past. After all, he had released "Decade", the triple album retrospective of his first ten years in 1977 and in recent years has spent much time working on a long-promised series of archival box sets, the first volume of which finally appeared at the end of 2009, and which was awarded a Grammy in 2010 for its art design. (Four further boxed set volumes have been planned.)

Although rust never sleeps, many of Young's best songs have paradoxically been meditations on the past. "Mansion On The Hill" is one of them, with lines such as "Psychedelic music fills the air, peace and love live there still" placing the song firmly in the late 1960s. The lyrics also refer to the murderous cult leader Charles Manson, whom Young had known in Topanga Canyon and whose activities had contributed to the death of the hippie dream.

DAYS THAT USED TO BE

"Days That Used To Be" again finds Young reminiscing about the idealism of the 1960s with clear references to his old colleagues in CSNY and was one of three songs written in a single session while on his boat the *W.N. Ragland*, sailing to Hawaii in the summer of 1988.

The melody is almost identical to Bob Dylan's 1964 composition, "My Back Pages", which Young himself was forced to concede when the similarity was pointed out by *Musician* magazine. "It's the same melody on three or four notes and there's no doubt about that. But it lends itself to bringing you back there," he reasoned. "It's in keeping with what the song's about to have a nostalgic twist in it."

LOVE AND ONLY LOVE

Crazy Horse get to stretch out again on "Love and Only Love", another ten-minute epic full of squalling electric guitar interplay between Young and Sampedro. Young revealed that there were three takes of the song. "One's really fast, another really slow. The slow one is angelic, the upside of the song. The fast one is pretty much the upside, too. But the middle one – the one we used – there's a real battle going on. A battle between good and bad."

Even Johnny Rogan, the one critic who dissented from the euphoria that greeted the album, was forced to admit that the song at least contained "all the ingredients" of the classic Young and Crazy Horse formula.

MOTHER EARTH (NATURAL ANTHEM)

After his support for Reagan in the 1980s, in "Mother Earth (Natural Anthem)" Young rediscovers his radicalism as an environmental crusader. Musically the song is a cross between the traditional folk song "The Water Is Wide" and Jimi Hendrix's feedback-drenched guitar version of "The Star Spangled Banner", which he famously performed at the Woodstock festival in 1969.

The track was recorded live at a *Farm Aid* benefit concert in April 1990 in Indianapolis and Young later explained his commitment to the ecological cause. "The environment is really important to me, at least for me to do my part, as much as I can to keep the ball rolling for the planet," he said. "What we are talking about is the Earth being raped and governments not coming to its defence and even being on the opposite side of the fence. I consider myself to be a citizen of Planet Earth first and a citizen of whatever country second."

Sentiments such as these did much to cheer those fans who had been sickened by the seemingly narrow-minded patriotic conservatism that he was spouting in the 1980s. It was also fitting that he chose to premiere the song live in a one-off CSNY reunion show in March 1990 to raise funds for the band's former drummer Dallas Taylor, who was suffering from liver disease.

HARVEST MOON

Recorded	September 1991 to February 1992, Woodside and Hollywood, California.
Produced by	Neil Young, Ben Keith
Musicians	The Stray Gators: Neil Young (vocals, guitar, banjo-guitar, piano, pump organ, vibes), Kenny Buttrey (drums), Tim Drummond (bass, marimba, broom), Ben Keith (pedal steel guitar, dobro, bass marimba, vocals), Spooner Oldham (piano, pump organ, keyboards). Additional personnel: Linda Ronstadt, James Taylor, Nicolette Larson, Astrid Young, Larry Cragg (vocals).

UNKNOWN LEGEND
FROM HANK TO HENDRIX
YOU AND ME
HARVEST MOON
WAR OF MAN
ONE OF THESE DAYS
SUCH A WOMAN
OLD KING
DREAMIN' MAN
NATURAL BEAUTY

THE GULF WAR, THE FIRST TELEVISED CONFLICT, FORMED THE BACKDROP TO THE WIDELY ACCLAIMED *SMELL THE HORSE* TOUR.

The ghost of *Harvest*, Young's most commercially successful album, had haunted him ever since its release in 1972. The album had created what he regarded as a false impression of him as a gentle, wistful singer-songwriter to rank alongside the likes of James Taylor and Jackson Browne. Although there had been further acoustic records, notably 1978's *Comes A Time*, he spent much of the next 20 years attempting not to follow-up his most successful release. It was a considerable surprise, therefore, when he let it be known in 1992 that he was assembling an album that he openly referred to as *Harvest Two*.

In part, the decision was forced by circumstances. Following the release of *Ragged Glory*, Young and Crazy Horse had taken to the road on the *Smell The Horse* tour. The Gulf War was raging on television screens every night and the conflict half way across the other side of the world seemed to inject a new intensity into the band's playing. The tour was recorded for the live double album *Weld*, the conflict going on in the Middle East reflected by the band's "Gulf War" version of Bob Dylan's "Blowing In The Wind", complete with air raid sound effects. An alternative version of the package also included a third CD, *Arc*, a composition of feedback, guitar noise, and vocal fragments realized from various shows on the tour – a new interest of Young's undoubtedly resulting from the influence of the tour's support band, Sonic Youth.

The tour and the excessive volume at which Crazy Horse played had taken their toll, however. Young's hearing was temporarily damaged (he later revealed he was suffering from tinnitus) and he was simply not physically capable of making another loud rock'n'roll record. "I made *Harvest Moon* because I didn't want to hear any loud sounds," he told *Mojo* several years later. "I still have a little bit of tinnitus but fortunately now I'm not as sensitive to loud sounds as I was for a year after the mixing of *Weld*."

A pastoral acoustic album also appeared to reflect his personal mood. It was time for peace after the war. "The next one's very, very quiet, so quiet you can really get up close to it. There's nothing angry or violent about this new music. It's about relationships and feelings. There's a lot of love in it," he told Nick Kent prior to the album's release.

Then he actually uttered the H-word. "It certainly sounds like the sequel to *Harvest*. I have no problem with that, though. I'm not backing away from that side of me any more," he said. And once he'd uttered the word, it was as if a weight had been lifted. "It's so obvious this next record is *Harvest Two*," enthused the man who had spent most of his career insisting that if he ever repeated himself it would be artistic death.

"When you hear it you'll think, 'Damn, he's finally made that follow-up to *Harvest*. All of 20 years later!' 'When's the next *Harvest* coming out?' Farmers have been asking me that for years," he joked. He even got together the Stray Gators, who had played on *Harvest* in 1972, as well as arranger Jack Nitzsche and even James Taylor and Linda Ronstadt, who had sung backing vocals on "Heart Of Gold".

However, by the time *Harvest Moon* was released in November 1992, Young had grown more wary about the comparison. Perhaps he was worried that the critics would think version two was not up to the standard of its predecessor and point to the lack of a song with the commercial impact of "Heart of Gold". Whatever the reason, he soon slipped into denial. "This is not *Harvest Two*," he insisted to the Radio One disc jockey Johnnie Walker, in complete contradiction of what he had told Nick Kent only months earlier. "They only compared it to *Harvest* because *Harvest* was a big success and this has 'Harvest' in the title. There are obvious things to connect up the two. But without *Harvest* this would still be *Harvest Moon* and stand on its own. Any connection with the past is a bonus."

If so, it was a very substantial bonus, producing his first British top ten album since *Harvest* itself and his highest-placed American album since 1979's *Rust Never Sleeps*. It was, as *Mojo*'s reviewer put it, quite simply, "the best record yet made by a middle-aged rock star about getting your life together."

UNKNOWN LEGEND

We knew of Young's attraction for girls in black leather on Harley-Davidsons from the dire "Motorcycle Mama" on 1978's *Comes A Time*. "Unknown Legend" dates from around the same time but is a far superior song. The figure is a composite of different woman and the first line "she used to work in a diner" suggests Young may be thinking back to the late 1960s and his first wife Susan Acevado whom he met in the café she owned in Topanga Canyon. The portrait is highly idealized with its images of wind-blown, long-haired blondes on the desert highway, although the verse about the "unknown legend" now "dressin' two kids" but who retains "the far-away look in her eyes" sounds like a picture of Young's wife Pegi, to whom the album is dedicated.

"It's inspired by some people I know and some people I don't know," was the closest Young would agree to be pinned down when asked about the song by Johnnie Walker. "They're just pictures, people's lives. A lot of the common thing is survival, not losing what it is you were when you were young, but take it with you into your own age. Don't leave it behind."

JIMI HENDRIX – THE GUITAR GOD IS STILL REVERED FOUR DECADES AFTER HIS DEATH.

FROM HANK TO HENDRIX

The title suggests a journey through rock'n'roll's back pages in the style of Rick Nelson's song "Garden Party". In fact, "From Hank To Hendrix" is a highly personal song about an enduring relationship to which the music of Hank Marvin and the Shadows (and conceivably Hank Williams) and Jimi Hendrix and all points in between is merely the soundtrack. The song appears to be addressed to Pegi, although there's a sharp jolt in the third verse, which finds the couple "headed for the big divorce, California style".

Young brushed questions about the reference aside when asked. "The divorce is never mentioned again," he pointed out. "It's just another element of the relationship."

YOU AND ME

Young had first sung the lines "I was thinking of you and me making love beneath the tree and now I wonder could it be" in concert in 1971. The lyric was used as a prelude to another song and the fragment was never completed. Two decades later he returned to the verse and completed the composition as "You And Me".

The song's theme, Young explained, was similar to "Unknown Legend". "It's about relationships and longevity and keeping the spark. You don't have to lose it because you're growing older," he told Johnnie Walker. "Our whole generation is at this point when they're starting to wonder whether they're too old to feel any more. You can. It's all still there, if you let it. That seems to be a theme that comes through in a few songs."

"I MADE HARVEST MOON *BECAUSE I DIDN'T WANT TO HEAR ANY LOUD SOUNDS."*

Nicolette Larson, last heard on *Comes A Time*, returns on backing vocals and the following year joined Young for his MTV *Unplugged* appearance. She died tragically in 1997.

HARVEST MOON

The same theme of lasting relationships and keeping the spark informs the title track, a dreamy tune bathed in gentle moonlight and Ben Keith's Hawaiian-style steel guitar. There's nothing deep or profound about "Harvest Moon" but it remains arguably the loveliest song on the album that bears its name.

WAR OF MAN

During the war with Iraq in 1991, Young was on tour with Crazy Horse. He watched the scenes of the world's first fully televised conflict avidly on CNN and was deeply moved. His own views were torn between support for the peace movement and a realization that the Iraqi leader Saddam Hussein was an evil tyrant who deserved little mercy. The effects were felt in his stage show, which took on a new intensity – and also in his songwriting.

"War Of Man" was written during the conflict and the refrain "no one wins" sums up the dilemma Young felt. However, the song's real concern is for the animals and birds destroyed in the crossfire rather than the human casualties.

The chorus of Linda Ronstadt and Nicolette Larson is joined by Astrid Young, Neil's half-sister.

ONE OF THESE DAYS

The nostalgia permeating the entire album becomes almost overwhelming on "One Of These Days", which finds Young contemplating a letter to "all the good friends I've known". Various musical characters are discernible in the lyrics. "That old country fiddler" is Rufus Thibodeaux who had been playing on-and-off as required on Young's albums since the aborted *Homegrown* sessions in Nashville in 1974. "Those ruff boys who play that rock'n'roll" are Crazy Horse. "I know I let some good things go" is a reference to CSNY's failure to make an album together in the 19 years that separated *Deja Vu* and 1989's much belated follow-up, *American Dream*.

"I've just begun to feel really for all my old bands, be they Crazy Horse, the Stray Gators, the International Harvesters and the Blue Notes, not to mention CSN for how they've been able to help me," he told Nick Kent. "I know of no other musician who's afforded the luxury of such a huge musical support network that will help me do what I feel I have to do."

He even admitted to pangs of guilt over how he had treated old colleagues. "I had to shit on a lot of people and leave a lot of friends behind to get where I am now," he told *Mojo*. "I had almost no conscience for what I had to do." The "letter" in "One Of These Days" (which we can only presume he never got around to writing because the song had done the job more effectively than the postal service) is both his apology and an expression of gratitude.

The song could easily have become over-sentimental but is saved by the beauty of the melody and the strength of the arrangement.

SUCH A WOMAN

Young's marriage to Pegi Morton is one of the most enduring in rock'n'roll. By the time *Harvest Moon* was released they had already been together for almost 15 years. She had inspired many of his songs over the years but none is more heartfelt and moving than the haunting piano ballad "Such A Woman".

Intriguingly, Nicolette Larson sings backing vocals on Young's tribute to the woman who succeeded her in his affections. Jack Nitzsche also returned to arrange the strings as he had done on *Harvest*. It's also interesting to compare the bombastic treatment on "A Man Needs A Maid" recorded on that earlier album with the subtler approach of "Such A Woman" two decades later.

OLD KING

A man needs a maid but a dog is his best friend. Having paid tribute to his wife on "Such A Woman" on "Old King" Young pays homage to his recently deceased tick hound Elvis – hence the title "Old King".

The dog had been a constant on-the-road companion for years and had almost become a star in his own right, prone to wandering on stage when Young was playing or barking from the wings.

DREAMIN' MAN

An otherwise unremarkable song, the gentle reverie of "Dreamin' Man" is only disturbed by the image of a loaded gun. Quite what it's doing is never clear as it's simply left lying there – like the divorce reference in "From Hank To Hendrix" – hinting at a bigger story and then failing to appear again.

The reference is incongruous because the rest of the song is exactly what you might expect from its title with Young hankering after "another time or place, another civilization", the kind of dreaming that had produced songs such as "Cortez The Killer" and "Like An Inca".

NATURAL BEAUTY

Recorded live at the Civic Auditorium in Portland, Oregon, the ten-minute "Natural Beauty" recalls the environmental concerns of "Here We Are In The Years" from Young's first solo album back in 1968. Whereas that song made the contrast between rural idyll and modern urban living with images of quiet country lanes contrasted with choked concrete highways, "Natural Beauty" contrasts "an anonymous wall of digital sound" with the natural cry of a new-born baby.

Towards the end of the song, Young introduces a sample from a world music album called *Dawn Chorus*, one of four in a series called *A Month In The Brazilian Rain Forest*, released on the Rykodisc label. The effect gives the track an ethereal feel more akin to Van Morrison's *Astral Weeks* rather than bearing any similarity to the work of such noted world music collaborators as Paul Simon or Peter Gabriel.

HARVEST MOON GAVE YOUNG HIS BIGGEST HIT IN OVER A DECADE.

SOLO DISCOGRAPHY

This listing does not include songs written and recorded with Buffalo Springfield, Crosby Stills, Nash and Young or The Stills-Young Band. Neither does it include compilations.

All songs composed by Young unless otherwise stated:

Neil Young
Reprise, January 1969
The Emperor of Wyoming; The Loner; If I Could Have Her Tonight; I've Been Waiting For You; The Old Laughing Lady; String Quartet from Whiskey Boot Hill; Here We Are In The Years; What Did You Do To My Life?; I've Loved Her So Long; The Last Trip To Tulsa.

Everybody Knows This Is Nowhere
Reprise, May 1969
Cinnamon Girl; Everybody Knows This Is Nowhere; Round and Round; Down By The River; (When You're On) The Losing End; Running Dry (Requiem For The Rockets); Cowgirl In The Sand.

After The Goldrush
Reprise, August 1970
Tell Me Why; After The Goldrush; Only Love Can Break Your Heart; Southern Man; Till The Morning Comes; Oh Lonesome Me (Don Gibson); Don't Let It Bring You Down: Birds; When You Dance I can Really Love; I Believe In You; Cripple Creek Ferry.

Harvest
Reprise, February 1972
Out On The Weekend; Harvest; A Man Needs a Maid; Heart Of Gold; Are You Ready For The Country; Old Man; There's A World; Alabama; The Needle and The Damage Done; Words.

Time Fades Away
Reprise, September 1973
Times Fades Away; Journey Through The Past; Yonder Stands The Sinner; L.A.; Love In Mind; Don't Be Denied; The Bridge; Last Dance.

On The Beach
Reprise, July 1974
Walk On; See The Sky About To Rain; Revolution Blues; For The Turnstiles; Vampire Blues; On The Beach; Motion Pictures; Ambulance Blues.

Tonight's The Night
Reprise, June 1975
Tonight's The Night; Speakin' Out; World On A String; Come On Baby Let's Go Downtown (Whitten/Young); Mellow My Mind; Roll Another Number (For The Road); Albuquerque; New Mama; Lookout Joe; Tired Eyes; Tonight's The Night Part Two.

Zuma
Reprise, November 1975
Don't Cry No Tears; Danger Bird; Pardon My heart; Lookin' For A Love; Stupid Girl; Drive Back; Cortez The Killer; Through My Sails.

American Stars'n'Bars
The Old Country Waltz; Saddle Up The Palomino; Hey Babe; Hold Back The Tears; Bite The Bullet; Star of Bethlehem; Will To Love; Like A Hurricane; Homegrown.

Comes A Time
Reprise, September 1978
Goin' Back; Comes A Time; Look Out For My Love; Lotta Love; Peace Of Mind; Human Highway; Already One; Field Of Opportunity; Motorcycle Mama; Four Strong Winds (Ian Tyson).

Rust Never Sleeps
Reprise, June 1979
My My Hey Hey (Out Of The Blue) (Young /Blackburn); Thrasher; Ride My Llama; Pocahontas; Sail Away; Powderfinger; Welfare Mothers; Sedan Delivery; Hey Hey My My (Into The Black).

Live Rust
Reprise, June 1979
Sugar Mountain; I Am A Child; Comes A Time; After The Goldrush; My My Hey Hey (Out Of The Blue); When You Dance I Can Really Love; The Loner; The Needle and The Damage Done; Lotta Love; Sedan Delivery; Powderfinger; Cortez The Killer; Cinnamon Girl; Like A Hurricane; Hey Hey My My (Into The Black); Tonight's The Night.

Hawks and Doves
Reprise, October 1980
Little Wing; The Old Homestead; Lost In Space; Captain Kennedy; Stayin' Power; Coastline; Union Man; Comin' Apart At Every Nail; Hawks and Doves.

Re-Ac-Tor
Reprise, October 1981
Opera Star; Surfer Joe and Moe The Sleaze; T-Bone; Get Back On It; Southern Pacific; Motor City; Rapid Transit; Shots.

Trans
Geffen, January 1983
Little Thing Called Love; Computer Age; We R In Control; Transformer Man; Computer Cowboy (aka Syscrusher); Hold On To Your Love; Sample and Hold; Mr Soul; Like An Inca.

Everybody's Rockin'
Geffen, August 1983
Betty Lou's Got A New Pair Of Shoes (Bobby Freeman); Rainin' In My Heart (Moore/West); Payola Blues(Young/Keith); Kinda Fonda Wanda (Young/Drummond); Jellyroll Man; Bright Lights Big City (Jimmy Reed); Cry Cry Cry; Mystery Train (Phillips/Parker); Everybody's Rockin.

Old Ways
Geffen, August 1985
The Wayward Wind (Lebowski/Newman); Get back To The Country; Are There Any More Real Cowboys?; Misfits; California Sunset; Old Ways; My Boy; Bound For Glory; Where Is The Highway Tonight?

Landing On Water
Geffen, July 1986
Weight Of The World; Violent Side; Hippie Dream; Bad News Beat; Touch The Night; People On The Street; Hard Luck Stories; I Got A Problem; Pressure; Drifter.

Life
Geffen, July 1987
Mideast Vacation; Long Walk Home; Around The World; Inca Queen; Too Lonely; Prisoner Of Rock'n'Roll; Cryin' Eyes; When Your Lonely Heart Breaks; We Never Danced.

This Note's For You
Reprise, April 1988
Ten Men Workin'; This Note's For You; Coupe de Ville; Life

In The City; Twilight; Married Man; Sunny Inside; Can't Believe Your Lyin'; Hey Hey; One Thing.

Eldorado (Japan only)
Reprise, March 1989
Cocaine Eyes; Don't Cry; Heavy Love; On Broadway (Leiber & Stoller); Eldorado.

Freedom
Reprise, October 1989
Rockin' In The Free World; Crime In The City (Sixty To Zero Part One); Don't Cry; Hangin' On A Limb; Eldorado; The Ways Of Love; Someday; On Broadway (Leiber & Stoller); Wrecking Ball; No More; Too Far Gone; Rockin' In The Free World.

Ragged Glory
Reprise, September 1990
Country Home; White Line; Fuckin' Up; Over and Over; Love To Burn; Farmer John (Don & Dewey); Mansion On The Hill; Days That Used To Be; Love and Only Love; Mother Earth (Natural Anthem).

Arc/Weld
Reprise, October 1991
Hey Hey My My (Into The Black); Crime In The City; Blowin' In The Wind (Dylan); Welfare Mothers; Love To Burn; Cinnamon Girl; Mansion On The Hill; Fuckin' Up; Cortez The Killer; Powderfinger; Love and Only Love; Rockin' In The Free World; Like A Hurricane; Farmer John; Tonight's The Night; Roll Another Number; Arc.

Harvest Moon
Reprise, November 1992
Unknown Legend; From Hank To Hendrix; You and Me; Harvest Moon; War Of Man; One Of These Days; Such A Woman; Old King; Dreamin' Man; Natural Beauty.

Unplugged
Reprise, June 1983
The Old Laughing Lady; Mr Soul; World On A String; Pocahontas; Stringman; Like A Hurricane; The Needle and The Damage Done; Helpless; Harvest Moon; Transformer Man; Unknown Legend; Look Out For My love; Long Many You Run; From Hank To Hendrix.

Sleeps With Angels
Reprise, September 1994
My Heart; Prime Of Life; Driveby; Sleeps With Angels; Western Hero; Change Your Mind; Blue Eden; Safeway Cart; Train Of Love; Trans Am; Piece Of Crap; A Dream That Can Last.

Mirror Ball
Reprise, June 1995
Song X; Act Of Love; I'm The Ocean; Big Green Country; Truth Be Known; Downtown; What Happened Yesterday; Peace and Love (Young/Vedder); Throw Your Hatred Down; Scenery; Fallen Angel.

Dead Man
Vapor, February 1996
Music from and inspired by Jim Jarmusch's film.
Broken Arrow
Reprise, July 1996
Big Time; Loose Change; Slip Away; Changing Highways; Scattered (Let's Think About Livin'); This Town; Music Arcade; Baby What You Want Me To Do (Jimmy Reed).

Year Of The Horse
Reprise, June 1997
When You Dance; Barstool Blues; When Your Lonely Heart Breaks; Mr Soul; Big Time; Big Time; Pocahontas; Human Highway; Slip Away; Scattered; Danger Bird; Prisoners Of Rock'n'Roll; Sedan Delivery.

Silver and Gold
Reprise, April 2000
Good To See You; Silver and Gold; Daddy Went Walkin'; Buffalo Springfield Again; The Great Divide; Horseshoe Man; Red Sun; Distant Camera; Razor Love; Without Rings.

Road Rock Vol 1
Reprise, November 2000
Cowgirl In The Sand; Walk On; Fool For Your Love; Peace Of Mind; Words; Motorcycle Mama; Tonight's The Night; All Along The Watchtower (Dylan).

Are You Passionate?
Reprise, April 2002
You're My Girl; Mr Disappointment; Differently; Quit (Don't Say You Love Me); Let's Roll; Are You Passionate?; Goin' Home; When I Hold You In My Arms; Be With You; Two Old Friends; She's A Healer.

Greendale
Reprise, August 2003
Falling From Above; Double E; Devil's Sidewalk; Leave The Driving; Carmichael; Bandit; Grandpa's Interview; Bringin' Down Dinner; Sun Green; Be The Rain.

Prairie Wind
Reprise, September 2005
The Painter; No Wonder; Falling Off The Face Of The Earth; Far From Home; It's a Dream; Prairie Wind; Here For You; This Old Guitar; He Was The King; When God Made Me.

Living With War
Reprise, May 2006
After The Garden;
Living With War; The Restless Consumer; Shock and Awe; Families; Flags Of Freedom; Let's Impeach The President; Lookin' for a Leader; Roger And Out; America The Beautiful.

Living With War: In The Beginning
Reprise, November 2006
"Stripped down" version of *Living With War,* featuring band recordings without overdubs. The album drops "Amercia The Beautiful".

Chrome Dreams II
Reprise, October 2007
Beautiful Bluebird; Boxcar; Ordinary People; Shining Light; The Believer; Spirit Road; Dirty Old Man; Ever After; No Hidden Path; The Way.

Fork In The Road
Reprise, April 2009
When Worlds Collide; Fuel Line; Just Singing a Song; Johnny Magic; Cough Up the Bucks; Get Behind the Wheel; Off the Road; Hit the Road; Light a Candle; Fork in the Road.

Dreamin' Man Live 92
Reprise, December 2009
Dreamin' Man; Such a Woman; One Of These Days; Harvest Moon; You And Me; From Hank To Hendrix; Unknown Legend; Old King; Natural Beauty; War Of Man.

INDEX

The publishers would like to thank the following sources for their kind permission to reproduce the pictures in this book:

Corbis: Bettmann: 43, 71, 83, 104, 120, 122; / Archivo Icongrafico: 91; /Ric Ergenbright: 47; / Dave G. Houser: 26; /David Muench: 111; /Neal Preston: 69, 107, 148; /Roger Ressmeyer: 115; /

Getty Images: 8; /Redferns: 3, 8, 14, 16, 20, 24, 35, 47, 49, 51, 56, 62, 137, 152, 162-163, 165, 187

LFI: 5, 13, 53, 85, 174; /Mike Hashimoto: 96

Retna: 30; /David Ellis: 80; /Peter Figen: 177; / Beth Gwinn: 97; /Tim Jarvis: 128; /Neal Preston: 77; /Aaron Rapoport: 141, 143, 157; /Chris Dooren: 112

Rex Features: 39, 59, 65, 89, 98, 100, 108, 126, 167, 181; /Harry Goodwin: 183; /Robin Platzer: 146; /Sipa Press/Alan Copeland; /Stills: 86; /Ton Farington: 125

Every effort has been made to acknowledge correctly and contact the source and/or copyright holder of each picture, and Carlton Books Limited apologises for any unintentional errors or omissions, which will be corrected in future editions of this book.